P9-BVG-718

ON THE ROAD TO TARA

ON THE

ROAD TO TARA

The Making of
GONE WITH THE WIND

Aljean Harmetz

HARRY N. ABRAMS, INC., PUBLISHERS

Editor: Adele Westbrook
Art Director: Samuel N. Antupit
Designer: Liz Trovato

Library of Congress Cataloging-in-Publication Data

Harmetz, Aljean.
On the road to Tara: the making of
Gone with the wind/Aljean Harmetz.
p.   cm.
Includes bibliographical references and index.
ISBN 0–8109–3684–4 (clothbound). —
[1. Gone with the wind (Motion picture)]   I. Title.
PN1997.G59H36 1996
791.43'72—dc20   96–4106

Published in 1996 by Harry N. Abrams, Incorporated,
New York
A Times Mirror Company

Front cover: *Top:* Detail of revised page of the final
shooting script for *Gone With the Wind,* where Rhett leaves
Scarlett. *Bottom left:* Detail of scene rendering drawn by
Dorothea Holt, showing Scarlett and Ashley in the
Twelve Oaks Library. *Bottom right:* A rare "D" style poster
for *Gone With the Wind.* (Collection Dennis A. Shaw
and James Tumblin)

Back cover: *Top:* Vivien Leigh in a hair and makeup still,
January 1939. *Bottom left:* Costume sketch for the
famous dress made from Tara's green velvet curtains.
Bottom right: Detail of watercolor sketch showing
the fields of Tara with the house in the background.

*The watercolor sketches on pages 1 to 13 were drawn
during the two years of preparation for* Gone With
the Wind. *Some, like the sketch by William Cameron
Menzies on pages 12–13, were simply early attempts to create
an environment. Others, like the detail from a seven-panel
storyboard of Rhett and Scarlett's flight from Atlanta on
page 1, were intended as blueprints for the cameraman and
director. Dozens of battle sketches, including the drawings on
pages 2–3 and 8–9, became unnecessary once it was decided
that the movie would only show the effects of the Civil War on
the South rather than the war itself. The scene renderings of
the church turned into a hospital on pages 10–11 and the
Tara servants arriving at Scarlett's grand house in Atlanta on
pages 6–7 mirror scenes in the movie.*

CONTENTS

Metro Goldwyn Mayer

présente
une production
DAVID O. SELZNICK

AUTANT
EN EMPORTE LE VENT

d'après le roman de *MARGARET MITCHELL*

avec

CLARK GABLE
VIVIEN LEIGH
OLIVIA DE HAVILLAND
LESLIE HOWARD

Couleurs par TECHNICOLOR

Réalisation de **VICTOR FLEMING**
musique de MAX STEINER

(Un film "*DAVID O. SELZNICK INTERNATIONAL*")

AFFICHES GAILLARD - PARIS - Dépôt légal ⁴⁵/₂ (23.585)   Imprimé en FRANCE

PROLOGUE

The two black limousines drove east through the orange groves. Movie studios always favored black limousines—it was important to appear important—but, in a September heat wave, black was a bad choice. At 5:00 P.M. on September 9, 1939, the temperature was still over 90, and there would be no air conditioning in cars for another fourteen years.

The heat inside the limousines was figurative as well as literal. The first car held fifty cans of motion picture film—separate sound and picture reels of the most expensive, most awaited movie Hollywood had ever made. According to a poll taken a few months earlier, fifty-six million people were interested in seeing *Gone With the Wind*. But audiences—then as now—are fickle. Fifty-six million people could quickly lose interest in a bad movie. And, for months, Hollywood insiders had been calling *Gone With the Wind* "The White Elephant" and "David's folly."

David was David O. Selznick, the rumpled, thirty-seven-year-old producer with bad eyes and hundred volt charm who sat in the back seat of the second car. As usual, Selznick's freshly pressed trousers looked as though he had slept in them, and the huge, flat feet that kept him constantly off balance took up too much space. "A big, huggy bear of a man," someone had called him, but the word that was most often used was "obsessive." He had bet his studio and $4 million he didn't have on the cans of film riding in the car ahead to a destination he didn't know.

Facing page: a rare French first release poster (Collection Dennis A. Shaw and James Tumblin). Above: The "D" style one-sheet, one of four posters used in 1939, is also rare because the image didn't appeal to theater owners, and most of the "D" style posters were destroyed (Collection Dennis A. Shaw and James Tumblin). Although Vivien Leigh was given second billing on the screen, the posters listed her fourth and read, "presenting Vivien Leigh as Scarlett O'Hara." In a memo to the movie's distributor on November 3, 1939, David Selznick wrote, "I think that Gable and Leigh are further set off by the names Rhett Butler and Scarlett O'Hara respectively in connection with their names; and I further think that the prominent use of these character names is important from a showmanship standpoint as they are almost as well known as the name of the book." In December 1995, a different style one-sheet sold at Christies in New York for $11,000.

If Selznick had been told where they were going, all Hollywood would have shown up at this first—secret—preview of *Gone With the Wind*. If Selznick would later be canonized as the greatest producer of Hollywood's golden age, he was also a child who couldn't keep a secret. "David would have told all his friends about it," Hal Kern, Selznick's film editor, said. So Kern, who was making $275 a week editing *Gone With the Wind*, had sent the studio boss home in mid-afternoon. And Selznick had waited in his big Beverly Hills house for the most important night of his life to begin.

Hindsight is perfect, and everyone knows how the story ends. Besides, $4 million is nothing today. You can't even buy a decent star for $4 million. Fifty-seven years ago, Hollywood was a different country. Selznick paid M-G-M $117,917 for Clark Gable. Vivien Leigh cost him $28,000. *Idiot's Delight*, the film Gable finished a few weeks before he started *Gone With the Wind*, was made for $1,519,000. Warner Bros.'s lavish *Adventures of Robin Hood* cost $2,033,000; and just under $2 million was spent on Irving Thalberg's personal production of *Mutiny on the Bounty*, M-G-M's most expensive movie before *The Wizard of Oz*, which was in production at the same time as *Gone With the Wind* and cost a breathtaking $2,777,000.

There is another way to look back. If it were made today with equivalent stars, sets, and special effects, *Gone With the Wind* would cost $100 million. And nearly everything that was written about *Waterworld* in the summer of 1995 could have been said about *Gone With the Wind*: Cost overruns, lavish spending, studio executives who began the movie with an incomplete script, and a 100 day production schedule that ballooned to 193 days.

The results, of course, were different. By the time the summer of 1995 was over, *Waterworld* was barely remembered. Fifty-seven years after that first preview, *Gone With the Wind* is still America's most famous movie.

But the future, being the future, was shrouded as the limousines headed inland to Riverside, and the air inside the cars got hotter because they had turned their backs on the Pacific Ocean and were driving toward the desert. "For us, the preview which had been a goal for so long now loomed as a threat," David's wife, Irene Mayer Selznick, wrote in her autobiography. "It could spell the end of everything in a few hours." The heat was "searing," she remembered more than forty years later, and David—galloping to victory or ruin—spent the journey sitting on the edge of his seat.

Selznick was probably hyped up on Benzedrine. He popped the pills like candy. Benzedrine gave him energy, not that he needed more energy. People were always saying Selznick was the most energetic man they had ever met. Wilbur Kurtz, the staid historian who came from Atlanta to be the technical advisor on *Gone With the Wind*, wrote in his diary after their first meeting that Selznick was a man "extruding energy." Benzedrine also kept Selznick awake during the weeks that he and his two film editors tore the film apart every morning and stitched it together again before they staggered out of the cutting room at 2:00 A.M. Irene could understand David's use of amphetamines during the months that *Gone With the Wind* put their house and their marriage "under siege." What she could never understand was why David took Benzedrine on Sunday to be able to play as hard as he worked.

Around 8:00 P.M., the limousines parked in front of the Fox Theater in Riverside. To avoid movie-wise audiences, sneak previews were usually held in cities fifty miles outside of Los Angeles. Kern had probably sounded out a few theater owners in advance, but it would have imperiled the secrecy to make complete arrangements earlier in the day. After they reached Riverside, Kern spent twenty minutes looking for a theater playing a compatible movie, a film that would draw an audience eager to see *Gone With the Wind*; and the Fox was showing *Beau*

Geste starring Gary Cooper—who had come as close as anyone except Clark Gable to playing Rhett Butler—as a man whose honor forced him to join the French Foreign Legion. Nobody in the theater would see *Beau Geste* that Saturday night, but it was an era of double bills and the audience had already had half their money's worth watching Johnny Downs lead a band among the pineapples in one of the decade's ubiquitous B musicals, *Hawaiian Nights*.

Once a theater had been chosen, Selznick's manic energy took over. Selznick wasn't the chairman of Selznick International Pictures. That title belonged to the money man—his friend John Hay "Jock" Whitney—who shared the limousine with David and Irene. But SIP was, in every respect, David's studio, and *Gone With the Wind* was David's movie. He had hired and fired directors and cinematographers. He had hired and fired a dozen writers and then written half the second half of the movie himself. He had scrawled, "O.K. DOS," on costume sketches and set designs, and he had chosen Vivien Leigh to play Scarlett O'Hara—a choice that Hedda Hopper, Hollywood's second most powerful gossip columnist, had said would ruin the movie.

In this era when directors are supreme and only stars are powerful enough to challenge their tyranny, it is hard to realize how fully the great producers—Irving Thalberg, Darryl Zanuck, Walt Disney, Hal Wallis, Samuel Goldwyn, and David Selznick—shaped their pictures sixty years ago. "I can tell you the picture from beginning to end, almost shot for shot," Selznick had written to Jock Whitney the day before *Gone With the Wind* began production with a "final" script that was merely a collage of bits and pieces of scripts by half a dozen writers.

"As long as I survive the whole situation is well in hand," Selznick wrote, "the whole picture in my mind from beginning to end." The only thing Whitney had to be afraid of was "for me suddenly to be run down by a bus." The words were David's usual combination of exaggeration, hyperbole, and self-dramatization, but they were also true. If Selznick had slipped under the wheels of a bus the night before the movie started shooting, *Gone With the Wind* wouldn't have been *Gone With the Wind*.

Standing outside his theater in the heat of that September night, the manager of the Fox Riverside agreed to Hal Kern's conditions. He would go on stage and announce that a preview was replacing *Beau Geste*, but he could not name the picture that was being previewed. No one would be allowed to enter the theater once the preview started and anyone who left would not be allowed back in.

Selznick had insisted that *Gone With the Wind* have the biggest title of any movie ever made. The applause, said Kern, "was thunderous" as each gigantic word—GONE . . . WITH . . . THE . . . WIND—moved separately and majestically across the screen. The applause was equally thunderous four hours and forty three minutes later when the picture ended.

Selznick spent those hours dictating notes to Barbara Keon, the production secretary on *Gone With the Wind* who had traveled to Riverside in the limousine with Kern and the film. The notes survive among the 57,000 pounds of paper that form the Selznick Archive in the Harry Ransom Humanities Research Center at the University of Texas at Austin. "Tara Opening: Too long on Scarlett leaving verandah and walking away from house. Too much of Mammy at window." "BARBECUE: Can't hear 'India Wilkes!' from Scarlett on arrival. Bring up 'Melanie Hamilton!' from Scarlett greeting Melanie in hall. Play 'You handsome old thing you!' from Scarlett to Chas. in different angle. Add ft. to Scarlett's 'shimmy' line on stairs with Cathleen . . ." Shot by shot, Selznick tore his picture apart.

Even before the preview cards were turned in and tabulated, Selznick felt—he was too much of a showman not to feel—the passion in the audience's response to *Gone With the Wind*. A week later, he would send a message to Margaret Mitchell, the author of the novel, that "a

Left to right: John Hay Whitney, Irene Selznick, Olivia De Havilland, David O. Selznick, Vivien Leigh, and Laurence Olivier at the Los Angeles premiere of Gone With the Wind, *held at the Carthay Circle Theater on December 28, 1939 (Courtesy Daniel Mayer Selznick).*

```
                                          "GONE WITH THE WIND"
                                          Ben Hecht
                                          February 26, 1939

     OPENING TITLE

     (Over scenes of the South's yesterday, its fields,
     plantations, river boats, manor halls, negro quarters,
     hunting parties, belles dancing, et cetera; over these
     scenes come the words...)

There was a land of Cavaliers and Cotton Fields called the
old South....

A Civilization half dead and half fairy tale thrived in
this land.

It was a pretty and gallant world full of proud, gentle and
absurd people.

It was the last tableau of Feudal Days, the last ever to be
seen of Knights and their Ladies Fair, of Master and of Slave....

Look for it only in books for it is no more than a dream
remembered, a land gone with the wind....
```

Civilization

Above: Screenwriter Ben Hecht's revision of the movie's opening title. Below: David Selznick (left) and his brother Myron at Grauman's Chinese Theater for the premiere of Selznick's The Prisoner of Zenda *in 1937 (Courtesy L. Jeffrey Selznick). Myron, four years older and considerably tougher than David, was his mother's favorite. The oldest of the three Selznick brothers, Howard, was brain damaged, the result of a birth injury.*

good two-thirds" of the preview cards had "used such phrases as 'Greatest picture ever made,' 'Greatest picture since *The Birth of a Nation*,' 'Screen's greatest achievement of all times,' etc." Of 157 questionnaires, 104 said the movie was excellent, wonderful, grand, and great.

But *Gone With the Wind* wasn't good enough for Selznick. He would spend the rest of September, October, and much of November changing the special effects, reshooting scenes, dubbing dialogue the preview audience had found unclear, recutting and eliminating almost an hour from the film. "We'd have been on it six months more," Hal Kern said, "if it hadn't been for Atlanta."

The premiere of *Gone With the Wind* had been scheduled for December 15, 1939, in Atlanta, Georgia, where the film and the novel took place; eventually there was no more time to make changes.

By that mid-December premiere, World War II was three months old. America wouldn't enter the war until December, 1941, when the Japanese bombed Pearl Harbor, but everyone knew what was coming. One of the questions asked at the two sneak previews of *Gone With the Wind* was, "Do you think that any battle scenes should be added to the picture, or any fuller portrayal of the Civil War, its causes and developments?" The people who answered yes said they wanted more battles because of "present-day conditions." One said that the dialogue by Rhett and Ashley about the futility of war was very good. "Leave in all the horror of war scenes," one person wrote. "Right now war should be painted at its worst."

Occasionally, a movie is lucky enough to be made at a perfect moment. On the edge of a cataclysm, *Gone With the Wind* and its audience raced toward each other. Selznick had written a prologue to the movie and then given it to Ben Hecht, one of *Gone With the Wind*'s many screenwriters, to rewrite.

"Look for it only in books," the prologue ended.

"For it is no more than a dream remembered.

A Civilization gone with the wind."

The movie was speaking of the "Cavaliers and Cotton Fields" of the Old South, blown away by the wind of the Civil War. In 1939, audiences saw a different civilization on the verge of extinction and felt a different wind. Throughout World War II, *Gone With the Wind* played continuously in London. The Nazis banned the film, rightly seeing its characters' battle for a lost cause as subversive to their cause. When the war was over, European audiences embraced the movie as fervently as American audiences had already done. There was rescue in this epic romance of desperation and survival.

In 1939, as the budget of *Gone With the Wind* soared to $4,250,000, Selznick was warned that the movie would have to sell an unprecedented $10 million worth of tickets before it would be profitable. By December 1940, a year after it was released, the film had grossed $14 million. Defying the usual six weeks that movies lasted, *Gone With the Wind* would play in American theaters for a second year.

By 1967, when it lost its position as the top money-making film of all time to *The Sound of Music*, *Gone With the Wind* had sold nearly $150 million worth of tickets in the United States alone. That didn't count the millions from Europe and Asia, and it was well before the money started coming in from cable television and videotapes. If the money *Gone With the Wind* has earned so far from theatrical rentals alone were to be translated into 1995 dollars, the total would be a minimum of $1 billion.

David Selznick was dead by 1967. He died in 1965 from a damaged heart, and perhaps the heart was broken too. When he died the headlines said what he had often predicted they would —that death had come for the producer of *Gone With the Wind*. Too successful too soon,

Facing page, top: Clockwise from top left, Vivien Leigh, Laurence Olivier, David Selznick, George Cukor, Irene Selznick, John Hay "Jock" Whitney, and Merle Oberon at dinner at Hill Haven, Myron Selznick's lodge near Arrowhead, over New Year's 1939, just after Leigh was cast as Scarlett. The most important talent agent of his era, Myron became an agent to punish the studio heads who had forced his father out of the business (Courtesy Daniel Mayer Selznick). Bottom: David Selznick and director George Cukor in London in 1934 to research David Copperfield *(Courtesy L. Jeffrey Selznick). Above: Russell Birdwell, who was a police reporter on the* Los Angeles Examiner *when Selznick chose him to head the studio publicity department, directed the two-year search for an actress to play Scarlett O'Hara (The Fred A. Parrish Collection). Left: The climax, the finale, the Atlanta premiere (Photo: Photofest).*

Selznick had spent the rest of his life trying to repeat that triumph. He came closest a year after *Gone With the Wind* won its Academy Award as the best picture of 1939, when *Rebecca* was named the best picture of 1940. Even now, Selznick remains the only producer ever to win that award two years in a row. But his future was already being poisoned. *Gone With the Wind*—as important to its generation as *Birth of a Nation* had been to early movie audiences—would become his albatross.

The night of February 29, 1940, when *Gone With the Wind* won eight Academy Awards, was perhaps the most triumphant in Selznick's life. There were awards to Hal Kern and James Newcom for film editing, to Lyle Wheeler for art direction, to Ernest Haller and Ray Rennahan for color cinematography, to screenwriter Sydney Howard, to director Victor Fleming, to actresses Vivien Leigh and Hattie McDaniel, and the Oscar to David Selznick as producer of the best movie of 1939. If you add in the Thalberg award to Selznick for the quality of his movies and a special award to William Cameron Menzies for his production design on *Gone With the Wind*, the film earned an unprecedented ten Oscars—double the five which *It Happened One Night*, the previous champion, had taken home in 1934. "Welcome to this benefit for David Selznick," Bob Hope, the master of ceremonies, quipped at one point during the evening.

In the Academy archives, there are dozens of pictures taken that night. In photograph after photograph, David is laughing. Even when he tries to be solemn—one should be serious and humble when winning awards—he is betrayed by a grin tugging at the corners of his mouth. Some people give nothing away when they are photographed; they allow the camera's prying eye to see only the surface. But all of Selznick is in the pictures—the potent charm that made people forgive him even when he kept them waiting for hours or never showed up at all, the optimism that knew tomorrow would not only be another day but a better one, the enthusiasm that was like a river sweeping everyone along. A soft man, awkward and ungainly, six feet tall while most of the other studio heads were squat and short, he towered over everyone that night. He had made *Gone With the Wind*.

The irony is that the movie was created through Selznick's weaknesses as well as by his strengths. Selznick's almost fatal inability to make up his mind caused him to delay production long enough for Vivien Leigh to show up on the studio doorstep. The delay also whetted America's appetite; by 1939 half the country was waiting for the film. Selznick's extravagance, his insistence on the biggest and most splendid of everything, created a gargantuan tapestry which was suitable for this particular epic, although that same extravagance would doom many of his future films. He was reckless and a compulsive gambler, losing $10,000 a month at the Clover Club, and what was *Gone With the Wind* but the biggest gamble of his life, with his future and his studio tossed into the pot?

Most of Selznick's future gambles would not pay off. In 1939, however, he won more than even he could have imagined. They used to say that the sun never set on the British empire. It is doubtful whether the sun sets on a day when some cable system or television station or home videocassette player in some country hasn't shown *Gone With the Wind*.

David Selznick and Vivien Leigh celebrate Oscars for Best Picture and Best Actress (© Copyright of Academy of Motion Picture Arts and Sciences). Gone With the Wind's *competition for the Academy's top award included* Dark Victory, Goodbye, Mr. Chips, Love Affair, Mr. Smith Goes to Washington, Ninotchka, Of Mice and Men, Stagecoach, The Wizard of Oz, *and* Wuthering Heights. Gone With the Wind's *thirteen nominations were not matched until 1950 when* All About Eve *earned fourteen nominations, still an Academy record. It took twenty years for the film's eight Oscars to be topped by* Gigi, *which won nine in 1958.*

When Gone With the Wind *opened in New York in December 1939, the movie critic of* The New York Times, *Frank Nugent, wrote, "Anyway, 'it' has arrived at last, and we cannot get over the shock of not being disappointed." The film did not disappoint members of the Academy of Motion Picture Arts and Sciences either. Clockwise from top left: Selznick picks up Victor Fleming's award for Best Director from presenter Mervyn LeRoy; Fleming was home ill. The 1,200 Academy members and guests who crowded into the Coconut Grove in the Ambassador Hotel for the awards dinner knew some of the winners in advance since the* Los Angeles Times *published the story before the banquet was over. Selznick is given the Irving Thalberg award for "the most consistent high quality of production during 1939." Hattie McDaniel, the first African-American ever to attend an Academy banquet, wore a garland of gardenias and got the biggest ovation of the evening when she accepted her award as supporting actress. The picture of Fleming receiving his Oscar was staged a few days later. (All photos © Copyright of Academy of Motion Picture Arts and Sciences)*

RETAKE
ALREADY
SHOT

Scarlett

I don't believe it!
    (she flies off on a run)

Gerald (calling after her)
Where are you off to? Scarlett!

here - here!

The authority of his voice stops her.

~~Gerald (with dawning realization)~~
~~Daughter! Look at you...Is it a spectacle you've~~ been making *of yourself*
of yourself? Running after a man who's not in love with you
when you ~~could~~ *might* have any of the bucks in the County?

(She turns away from him)

Scarlett

I haven't been running after him. It's A It's just a surprise ~~to me~~ *That's*

~~Gerald~~
~~It's lying you are!~~
    ~~(he peers at her stricken face and softens. He lifts~~
    ~~her chin kindly and changes his tone)~~
~~Oh, I know Ashley's been squiring you about a few times,~~
~~Missy, but you're young and there's lots of other beaux.~~

~~Scarlett~~
~~I don't want any other beaux!~~
X-X-X-X-X-X-X-X-X-X-X-X-X-X-X-X-X-X-X-X-X-X-X-X-X-X-X-X-

Gerald

~~TO BE~~
~~SHOT~~

Gerald
Now don't be jerkin' your chin at me.
    (he follows her, puts his arm around her)
If Ashley wanted to marry you, t'would be with misgivings I'd
say "yes." I want my girl to be happy...and ~~you wouldn't~~ be
happy with him.   *you're not*

Scarlett
~~Oh,~~ I would, I would!

Gerald
"But what
difference does
it make who's
you marry?"

Gerald (shaking his head)
Only when like marries like ~~can~~ there be any happiness. And
the Wilkeses are different from us...'Tis moonstruck they all
are. Let them marry their cousins and keep their books and
their ~~music~~ and such foolishness to themselves.
    operas

Scarlett
Oh, Pa, if I married him I'd change all that.

Gerald
Oh, you would, would you? No wife ~~has~~ ever changed a husband
yet...~~And~~ *But* what does it matter who you marry ~~so~~ long as he's
a Southerner and thinks like you?

Tears of frustration come into Scarlett's eyes. She bows
her head. Gerald takes her arm; they start walking again,
turning toward a rise of ground.

Gerald
And when I'm gone --
    (observes she is paying no attention)
~~Whisht, darlin'! Listen to me!~~ I'll leave Tara to you --

Scarlett
I don't want Tara! Plantations don't mean anything when --

Gerald (stops in his tracks, indignant)
Do you mean to tell me, Katie Scarlett O'Hara, that Tara -
that land doesn't mean anything to you?

CONTINUED:

Revised
What are you
about?
(He catches up
with her and
takes her by
the arm)
(with dawning
realization)
Have you

hs

SCRIPTS
Never Hire One Writer When Eleven Writers Will Do

I t took David Selznick six weeks to make up his mind to buy *Gone With the Wind*. Today, the movie rights would be gone in a weekend. Within twenty-four hours of the manuscript's arrival at the publisher, movie industry spies would run off half a dozen photocopies and slip them to producers. Someone as indecisive as Selznick would not be able to compete.

Selznick bought the rights for $50,000 on July 7, 1936. By that time the novel, which had been published in June, was selling out in bookstores all over the country. Jack Warner of Warner Bros. matched Selznick's offer—but he did so a few hours too late.

Although Selznick had been manipulated into buying *Gone With the Wind* by his New York story editor, Kay Brown, and he didn't actually read the book until it had sold half a million copies, book and producer were a match made in the movie land of happy endings. Selznick might have waited the rest of his life for a story that so satisfied his need for sweep, exuberance, and words, words, words.

Selznick and Darryl Zanuck of 20th Century-Fox were the two most literate studio heads—Zanuck had begun as a writer—but their taste in literature could not have been more different. Zanuck bid $35,000 for *Gone With the Wind* before Selznick bid $50,000, and he never raised his offer. It was contemporary stories with a social edge that intrigued Zanuck, although he was

Above: Sidney Howard, who would be given sole screenplay credit for Gone With the Wind, *was one of America's most important playwrights. He wrote for Hollywood whenever he needed money to write another play. In this February 22, 1936 photograph, Howard has just stepped off the 20th Century Limited. Facing page: This scene was revised on June 10, 1939, probably by David Selznick.*

shrewd enough to file off the sharpest edges. The big movie Zanuck was producing in 1939 was *The Grapes of Wrath*, and he had paid $100,000 for John Steinbeck's unsettling novel about Oklahoma farmers forced to abandon their land by drought and the Great Depression. Zanuck had already made *I Am a Fugitive From a Chain Gang*, and, a decade later, he would produce *Gentleman's Agreement*, the first studio movie whose subject was anti-Semitism. He would win the Thalberg award three times to Selznick's once.

For David Selznick, the best books were a century old, and the greatest author was Charles Dickens. In *Gone With the Wind*, Selznick would have Melanie read aloud from *David Copperfield* where Margaret Mitchell had chosen to have her read from *Les Miserables*. Selznick had already made movies of *David Copperfield*—it was among his best—and *A Tale of Two Cities*. He had also filmed *Anna Karenina*, *The Adventures of Tom Sawyer*, and, as his first film at Selznick International Pictures, *Little Lord Fauntleroy*. The stories that attracted Selznick were set in an atmosphere-drenched time past; they were spilling over with characters and activity, but he could still manage to find some way to enlarge the canvas.

In most cases, Selznick's virtues as a producer outweighed his faults. However, during the nearly three years it took to create a screenplay for *Gone With the Wind*, there was an uneven match between Selznick's creative instincts and his uncreative chaos. One has only to look at the box after box of *Gone With the Wind* scripts in the Selznick Archive to see how his need to trip himself up surpassed his creativity. Selznick discarded good scripts, hired unnecessary writers, and caused unnecessary delays.

Selznick lacked even the rudiments of self-discipline, and too much freedom was poisonous to him. Only at the very end—with the movie in production and further delay no longer possible—did creativity conquer chaos. During those last weeks, Selznick himself was responsible for ending the film with the physical reality of Scarlett's return to Tara; and it was his idea to have Scarlett hear the voices of Gerald O'Hara, Ashley, and Rhett directing her home. Without being false to the unhappy ending of the book, Selznick's ending was more emotionally satisfying and less bitter.

It was common in Hollywood—it is still common—for studios to use screenwriters as blotting paper. When one had soaked up all of the producer's ideas and been wrung out, there was always a clean sheet at hand. Unlike many other studio executives, Selznick did not lack taste or discrimination. However, he did not trust his own judgment, so he threw writers at a movie reflexively—hiring a new writer almost before he bothered to read what the previous writer had written. Eleven different screenwriters would be paid for their work on *Gone With the Wind* between the fall of 1936 and the summer of 1939; and Selznick would solicit the unpaid views of half a dozen others. Eventually there would be a filing cabinet full of scripts, Selznick's notes on the scripts, revisions based on Selznick's memos, various scenes polished by various writers, and Selznick's own rewrites of the writers' scenes. In the end, most of the dialogue and much of the structure would be taken intact from the novel, and the first writer Selznick hired, Sidney Howard, would receive sole screen credit.

Selznick considered Ben Hecht and Sidney Howard to be the two best screenwriters who were not under contract to a studio in 1936. When Margaret Mitchell refused his offer to adapt her own novel, Selznick hired Howard. But, even as he asked Howard to write the screenplay, Selznick must have known that he would use Hecht later as a pinch hitter.

Almost as soon as he hired Howard in the fall of 1936, Selznick became disturbed because Howard was intending to write the script on his Massachusetts farm. "I have never had much success with leaving a writer alone to do a script without almost daily collaboration with myself," Selznick fretted.

Handsome, a 1915 graduate of the University of California and a World War I pilot in France, Sidney Howard was America's second most respected playwright, outdone only by Eugene O'Neill. He had won the 1925 Pulitzer Prize for *They Knew What They Wanted*, which would have a second life three decades later as the musical *The Most Happy Fella*. He had made a smash play out of Sinclair Lewis's novel, *Dodsworth*, and then turned the play into an exceptional movie for Sam Goldwyn. "He was a born leader. His outstanding quality was that on very first meeting you knew he was adult in every sense of the word," said John Wharton, the lawyer who helped Howard and playwrights Robert E. Sherwood, Elmer Rice, Maxwell Anderson, and S. N. Behrman create their own producing organization in 1938, "His plays reflected this maturity."

Howard had first come to Hollywood in 1929, when Goldwyn paid him $10,000 to write the dialogue for Goldwyn's first talking picture, *Bulldog Drummond*. "Sidney Howard immediately grasped motion pictures. He genuinely had the knack," says Goldwyn's biographer, Scott Berg. "And Sam was a great admirer of literary talent. Almost every picture Howard and Sam did together was a success."

In 1936, Sidney Howard still owed $953 on his 1935 income taxes. And all his cash had gone into the 120-acre farm he had recently bought in Tyringham, Massachusetts. His need for Selznick's money would grow as his taxes and the farm expenses grew.

The treatment Howard sent to Selznick in December 1936 and the first draft he completed in February 1937 would be the basis of David O. Selznick's production of *Gone With the Wind*. But not until they had been buried under an avalanche of scripts, rewrites, and suggestions by Jo Swerling, Oliver Garrett, F. Scott Fitzgerald, Edwin Justus Mayer, John Van Druten, Ben Hecht, John Balderston, Winston Miller, Michael Foster, and John Lee Mahin, and had been rewritten several times by Howard and then by Selznick himself.

In his treatment Howard pruned characters, divided the story into seven main sequences, and eliminated Margaret Mitchell's flashbacks. He began his movie as the author had begun her novel, with the Tarleton twins and Scarlett sitting on the sunny porch at Tara; then he followed Mitchell's path through the first half of the story, emphasizing the O'Hara love for Tara and the other two love stories—Melanie and Ashley and Rhett and Scarlett. He ended the first half as the movie would, with Scarlett returning to Tara to find her mother dead and swearing, "As God is my witness, we're going to live through this, and when this war is over, I'm never going to be hungry again."

Howard added two things to the first half: a series of montages showing the ever more desperate plight of the South and a sequence that showed Rhett Butler running the Northern blockade. The montages would be in the final picture; Rhett in action would not.

Selznick's understanding of movies and movie audiences illuminates the letter he wrote Howard after studying the fifty-page treatment. ". . . I urge you very strongly indeed against making minor changes . . . These minor changes may give us slight improvements, but there will be five or ten million readers on our heads for them; where, for the most part, they will recognize the obvious necessity of our making drastic cuts. I feel, too, that we should not attempt to correct seeming faults of construction. I have learned to avoid trying to improve on success. One never knows what chemicals have gone to make up something that has appealed to millions of people, and how many seeming faults of construction have been part of the whole, and how much the balance would be offset by making changes that we in our innocence, or even in our ability, consider wrong."

Selznick was adamant that Rhett not be shown "doing his stuff as a blockade runner." He urged Howard to "abide by Miss Mitchell's failures as well as her successes, because I am frankly nervous about anybody's ability—even Miss Mitchell's—to figure out which is which. I think she herself might very well rewrite the book into a failure."

Howard answered Selznick with a warning of his own: "The tough part is the arrangement of the material. The book is written in a series of islands: good enough novel technique, but you have to produce a picture, not an archipelago. Where the islands are big enough, as, for example, the whole passage beginning with Melanie's baby and ending with the flight from Atlanta, we encounter no trouble. Where they are small, as, for example, Belle Watling's attempt to give money to the hospital, they can be fairly fussy."

When Howard turned in the first draft of his screenplay in February 1937, the playwright was willing—in fact, wanted—to come to California so that he could revise the script and move on to his new play, *The Ghost of Yankee Doodle*, which he was writing for Ethel Barrymore. But Selznick had trouble focusing on one thing. Howard was only one of dozens of observers who would note that Selznick had no sense of how to organize his time. It was as though David needed to create chaos. He was intending to have *Gone With the Wind* in production by December at a cost of no more than $1.5 million. Yet, during the early months of 1937, he was also trying to finish *A Star Is Born*, and he had had his fancy stolen away by *The Prisoner of Zenda*, in which he was starring Ronald Colman. When he sent for Howard in April, instead of discussing *Gone With the Wind*, Selznick immediately put him to work writing a love scene for *Zenda*.

Howard was by no means the first writer Selznick had ordered to write new love scenes for *Zenda*, and he plaintively asked his diary why Selznick didn't realize that the author, Anthony Hope, had written the novel a lot better than Selznick could. After he was told to rewrite the important ballroom scene in *Zenda*, Howard asked Selznick how he wanted it rewritten. "I don't know," Selznick responded. "I haven't read it yet."

So, at a cost to Selznick of $500 a day, Howard worked on his play and worried about his farm. He sent home instructions for planting ten new fruit trees—apples, pears, and plums—and negotiated buying more land. His debts were mounting. He already owed $165 for a crushed stone drive, and he was having a pipeline laid that would bring water to the barn, the vegetable garden, and the stable he was renovating. The excavating and piping would cost $1,650.

Eventually, Selznick got around to reading Howard's *Gone With the Wind* script. Howard's first draft would have made a six hour movie, but that was a deliberate choice by the playwright. "It is obvious that some radical amputations of book material will be obligatory," he wrote when he sent Selznick the script. "The book itself is so unwieldy that we shall, in my opinion, be safer if those amputations are made in a picture script. With all my study of the book (and I certainly know it better than anyone living except Miss Mitchell) I am not decided on what to cut out. . . . What you are getting, however, is *Gone With the Wind* reduced from a thousand to 250 pages. Weeding of dialogue and dead wood will take out another fifty. Then you and I use the axe and I sew up the wound."

Howard's letter pinpointed the problem which faced any writer who tried to adapt the novel: "I spent by far the greatest part of my time trying my damndest to get a sequence on the sufferings of the South during the early days of reconstruction. . . . I have failed on that thus far and I suspect that we shall all fail on it. Miss Mitchell's picture of the reconstruction does not involve either Scarlett or Rhett once Scarlett has left Tara. Scarlett marries Frank, gets her lumber mill and does very nicely except that a very dull collection of old southern friends don't approve of women in business. . . . Thus I have short-changed you on reconstruction by jumping from Scarlett's marriage to Frank to Frank's death. I might add that Frank would have been left out except for the fact that his death makes her marriage to Rhett so much more dramatic."

All the other writers would also fail to solve that difficulty in the novel.

Other choices were easier. Selznick and Howard both shied away from the dangerous Ku Klux Klan sequences. In 1937, African-Americans were still being lynched in the South, and the two men agreed that they could handle Scarlett's near-rape in Shantytown without calling in the Klan to avenge her. In Selznick's words, "A group of men can go out to 'get' the perpetrators of an attempted rape without having long white sheets over them." It would be another year, however, before Selznick understood the depth of black antagonism to the book.

Howard's daily letters to his wife, Polly, are a fever chart of his rising frustration. The mature man, the craftsman, was drowning in the undertow of the charming perennial boy for whom he worked.

Selznick had been brought up to think that everything he did was right. The spoiled son of a father who adored him, David was making decisions in his father's movie business at a salary of $750 before he was seventeen. Neither father nor son saw anything odd in the fact that until twenty-eight-year-old David married Irene Mayer, his father put him to bed every night.

Obsessive in every detail of making his movies, David was equivalently irresponsible in daily life. "I don't believe there were a dozen nights in the fifteen years we lived together that he got home at the hour he said he would," Irene Selznick wrote in her autobiography. He expected to be praised if he reached a dinner party no more than an hour late. "He carried no keys and knew no telephone numbers except the house and the studio. There was always someone around to help him—in a pinch he could call the studio switchboard. . . . He also didn't carry money, which was no inconvenience at all—to him."

Howard tried to cope.

April 22, 1937: "Selznick, a very nice and polite gent, has still to learn that there are several equally good ways to skin a cat. He has the same failing Thalberg had of seeing only his way and failing to realize that his way, filtered through author and director, may, eventually, prove less effective than the author's or director's way accepted by him."

April 26: "No one shows the slightest interest in *Gone With the Wind* and I am beginning to suspect that Selznick is not going to make it."

April 29: "My obligation terminates next Wednesday by which time I shall have earned practically nothing of the $37,500 I have collected. The only possible explanation I can find for the keeping of Cukor in New York is that Selznick cannot bear to let him and me work without interference."

By May 1, 1937, Selznick had left for New York; director George Cukor, who had been racking up a salary of $4,000 a week criss-crossing the country searching for a Scarlett O'Hara, and who would end up being paid $253,000 for a movie from which he was fired after fourteen days of shooting, had not been allowed to come to California to work with Howard. As Howard put it, while he sat uselessly in California for five weeks, Cukor sat uselessly a continent away.

Because of Selznick's constant changes of plans, Howard had postponed the production of *The Ghost of Yankee Doodle*. Now he either had to bail out of *Gone With the Wind* or resign from an exciting project offered by Goldwyn. "I am only too eager to ask Selznick to let me out," he wrote Sam Marx, Goldwyn's story editor, in June 1937 after he returned to Tyringham. Since it would be embarrassing for Goldwyn if Howard dumped *Gone With the Wind* for the airline story that he wanted to write, the playwright was back in Hollywood for Selznick in July. But, as he wrote Margaret Mitchell, "I am a bit of an agnostic on the subject of their ever getting down to work in my few years this side of the grave."

For a week in mid-July, Howard worked with Cukor in the morning and trimmed his script with Cukor and Selznick in the afternoon. Then Selznick decided to retake the ending of *The Prisoner of Zenda*. The only way Howard and Cukor could get Selznick to focus his attention on *Gone With the Wind* was for Howard to write *Zenda*'s new ending and for Cukor to shoot it.

Still, Howard was not unhappy, although he was homesick for farm, wife, children, and dogs. After a bad first marriage, he was genuinely happy with Polly. The work was going well too. The only difficulty, he wrote, was that Cukor "keeps screaming for more dialogue from the book and I keep screaming for more action in lieu of dialogue."

Cukor had begun as a stage director, and he and Howard shared a preference for understated and intimate scenes and a distaste for phony dramatic moments. So Selznick felt that the draft that was completed in August 1937, was not theatrical enough. Still, Selznick thought it was in good shape. "We have somewhere between two and three weeks work remaining to clean up script of GONE WITH THE WIND," he wrote Kay Brown. That final work, he assured her, would be done in the fall, when he and Cukor met with Howard in New York.

But nothing Selznick did was ever final. Sidney Howard was back in Hollywood in January 1938—more than a year after he had sent in his original treatment. Also in Hollywood—for the first time—was Atlanta historian Wilbur Kurtz whom Margaret Mitchell had recommended to Selznick as a technical advisor. According to Kurtz's journals, he was "parked in the Beverly Hills Hotel for no other reason than to be in contact with Sidney Howard." The script that Howard gave Kurtz over two-inch-thick steaks at the Cock and Bull restaurant was dated November 27, 1937.

Kurtz was entranced. Howard had managed to merge Margaret Mitchell's islands into continents. "Another magical touch," Kurtz wrote. "He takes three or four incidents, and groups them in a sequence—making unity out of a diversification." Among the things Kurtz admired was Howard's changing the route Scarlett took home to Tara with Melanie and her newborn baby so that they passed the ruined Twelve Oaks.

By the time Howard left Selznick's employ on February 2, with the screenplay supposedly completed, Kurtz had learned enough about Hollywood to be able to write, "The quickest way to get a laugh is to say something about a script being finished!"

Howard and Bill Menzies had been friends since 1929, when Menzies designed and Howard wrote *Bulldog Drummond* for Sam Goldwyn; and Howard came to Menzies's office to say goodbye. Kurtz was there, working with Menzies on sketches of Tara. For once, Kurtz wrote, Howard didn't seem mild and preoccupied. Instead he "orated" his "sardonic" last words: "Yes, I'm through. It's not a movie script. It's a transcription from the book. But what else could I do? The book is not designed for the movies. I just used Miss Mitchell's words and scenes."

Howard, who was paid a total of $84,834 for his work on *Gone With the Wind*, would come back to the studio. But not for more than a year. However, he didn't leave Hollywood right away. He couldn't afford to. He would make almost $100,000 in 1938, and nearly all of the money would go for back income taxes, his share of seed money for the Playwrights Producing Company, a herd of Jersey cows, and a barn to house them. So he simply moved a few miles east to work for Sam Goldwyn on *Transatlantic Flight*, which would never become a movie. Howard had written five or six drafts of *Gone With the Wind*, but he felt the script still had too much dialogue. A month later Selznick agreed with him, and Howard moonlighted seven or eight hours a week cutting the script.

Goldwyn was more tyrannical than Selznick, but his philosophy of screenwriting was considerably different. He bought the best literary talent he could find—Lillian Hellman, Ben

The word "Titles" is written in the top left hand corner of this scene rendering, implying that the plowed fields of Tara would be used as part of the montage of images behind the movie's opening credits.

Hecht, Robert E. Sherwood, and Sidney Howard—and, unlike Selznick, if Goldwyn trusted a writer he let him do his job. In Sherwood's Oscar winning script for *The Best Years of Our Lives*, for example, barely a word was changed by Goldwyn.

Selznick was incapable of keeping his hands off anything, and, since he thought of himself as a writer, he found other people's scripts irresistible. On several of his later movies—*Since You Went Away* (1944), *Duel in the Sun* (1946), and *The Paradine Case* (1947)—he would take screen credit for the scripts. Ben Hecht thought that Selznick, Zanuck, and Goldwyn were the brightest of the studio bosses. Hecht, who was usually inclined to cynicism, admiringly described Selznick as "a brilliant plotter" who could create "twenty different permutations of any given scene without stopping to catch his breath." In the case of *Gone With the Wind*, however, that agility with words and ideas was no help; it only added more material to the stew.

By 1938, Selznick was fixated on bringing Margaret Mitchell's novel to the screen as faithfully as possible. Always impressed by great literature, the man who had dismissed the book on May 25, 1936, as a "fine story" but one whose Civil War background made it likely to fail as a movie was now speaking of the book as a classic. Not only was *Gone With the Wind* a phenomenal popular success which had sold almost two million copies; it had also won the Pulitzer Prize for 1936. Among the books it defeated was William Faulkner's *Absalom, Absalom*.

Most of the scene renderings sketched by William Cameron Menzies, art director Lyle Wheeler, and their staff artists for Gone With the Wind *were watercolor drawings between thirty and thirty-six inches wide and twenty to thirty inches tall. Selznick wanted every scene sketched in the greatest possible detail, but he never reached his goal, which was what he called "a pre-cut film," in which every shot was drawn ahead of time.*

In his passion for accuracy, Selznick insisted that the fields of his Tara be plowed in curved rows, the technique used on North Georgia plantations to keep the rich soil from running into the river bottoms. A version of the scene sketched above can be seen under "Margaret Mitchell's Story of the Old South" in the movie's opening credits.

To make matters worse, month by month Selznick was changing his ideas about the scope and grandeur of the movie—something that is clear to anyone who reads through his memos.

In a message to be passed on to Sidney Howard immediately after he hired the playwright, Selznick wrote, "Wish that you would have a talk with him about not going overboard on size and expensive production scenes of the Civil War. . . . " In March 1937 he insisted that the movie would have a budget of $1,500,000 "if we have stars, and $1,250,000 if we have not. This should be more than ample if we don't go nuts." By September 1938, the budget was $2,800,000, and Selznick intended to make "the longest picture ever made."

The combination of Selznick's rising expectations, his determination to be faithful to the novel, and his disorganization was deadly. He had breakdowns made of the book and collated them with each screenplay. He circled the bits he liked from each of Howard's scripts and then rewrote those pieces into new scenes. Then he rewrote the scenes again. In the end, Selznick would say that he had written "the last half or two-thirds of the script without anybody's help," a considerable exaggeration.

Selznick's problems were not entirely of his own making. Margaret Mitchell always said that it would be impossible to turn her book into a movie. "It had taken me ten years to weave it as tight as a silk pocket handerchief," she wrote to Susan Myrick, a Georgia journalist who was one of *Gone With the Wind*'s technical advisers, after Myrick told her about the script difficulties. "If one thread were broken or pulled an ugly ravel would show clear through to the

The "WCM" signature in the bottom left corner means that Menzies drew this sketch — intended for a Tara montage — himself.

A tag in the upper right hand corner of this sketch by Dorothea Holt identifies it as Set No. 18, the exterior of Peachtree Street in Atlanta. Ms. Holt and Joseph McMillan "Mac" Johnson were the two artists most often used by Menzies and Wheeler, and their signatures are on numerous sketches for Gone With the Wind.

43

One of the smallest scene renderings, only thirteen by nineteen inches, this sketch shows Rhett and Scarlett. According to technical adviser Wilbur Kurtz, the ranches that supplied horses and buggies to the movie studios competed more fiercely than usual in 1939. "They all want in on GWTW," Kurtz wrote, "for the picture rates high as a horse and carriage opera." Other props that Kurtz scouted were army wagons, harness equipment, wooden tubs with proper stave handles, hospital beds, coffeepots for the barbecue at Twelve Oaks, and the slave bell at Tara.

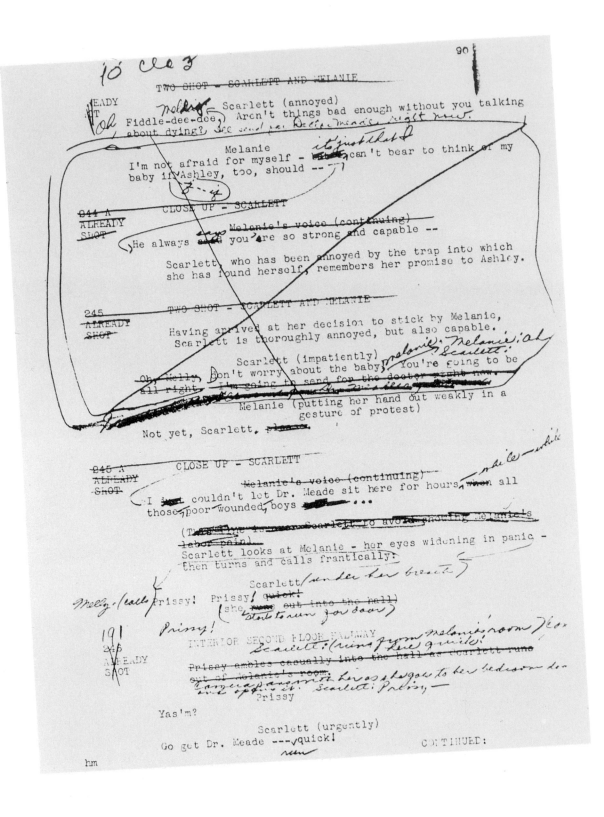

This is the final version of a scene between Scarlett and Melanie after Melanie has gone into labor. To keep track of revisions, each re-write was typed on a different color paper. The yellow paper means that these lines were re-written three times during the shooting of the movie.

other side of the material. Yet they would have to cut for a script, and when they began cutting they would discover they had technical problems they never dreamed about."

In August 1938, Selznick borrowed Clark Gable from M-G-M to play the role of Rhett Butler. It was the casting moviegoers had been demanding from the moment the book was published. But signing Gable meant that Selznick had to play by the rules of tidy, well-organized M-G-M. That studio would be using Gable for a picture in October (*Idiot's Delight*, adapted from Robert E. Sherwood's Pulitzer Prize-winning play) and would then deliver the actor to Selznick International Pictures no later than January 15, 1939.

The clock was finally ticking. The movie must go into production in January. And although Selznick had four drawers of a filing cabinet filled with script materials, he didn't have a script.

Selznick fled to Bermuda with several cartons of scenes and sequences and writer Jo Swerling. Margaret Mitchell had declined to accompany him. So had Sidney Howard. Polly Howard was expecting a baby October 1. (With a thoughtlessness that was typical of him, Selznick assured Howard that Polly would be able to travel by October 8.) Swerling was a bad third choice. He would be paid $1,250, but he was defeated by the masses of material.

"WILL REQUIRE DIALOGUE WRITER 'WIND' PREFERABLY STARTING ON MY ARRIVAL NEW YORK," Selznick telegraphed his lieutenant, Dan O'Shea, from Bermuda on November 11. "UNDERSTAND GARRETT'S PLAY TERRIBLE FLOP, SO SHOULD BE ABLE BUY HIM CHEAPLY. FIND OUT PRICE WEEK-TO-WEEK JOB ON 'WIND.' THIS APART FROM NEED OF DIALOGUE WRITER, AS WELL."

Oliver H. P. Garrett traveled west with Selznick on the *Super Chief* on November 28. Although Garrett was paid $14,792 and demanded a screen credit—which Selznick refused to give him—there is little of his work in the film. "Offhand I doubt that there are ten original words of Garrett's in the whole script," Selznick wrote O'Shea when he was worried that Garrett might make a public fuss. "As to construction, this is about 80% my own, and the rest divided between Jo Swerling and Sidney Howard, with Hecht having contributed materially to the construction of one sequence."

Garrett, who had been preceded by two screenwriters, was succeeded by eight. The starting date of *Gone With the Wind* had been pushed back to January 23, 1939, and then to January 26. During January and February, Edwin Justus Mayer ($4,167), John Balderston ($1,750), Michael Foster ($1,675), John Van Druten ($7,195), Winston Miller ($893), Ben Hecht ($5,000), John Lee Mahin ($1,000), and F. Scott Fitzgerald were put to work on the script. Fitzgerald, who was budgeted for $7,500 but would only be paid $2,904, was on loan from M-G-M to examine the script and polish the dialogue. Two dozen memos from Fitzgerald remain in Selznick's script files and, in most of them, Fitzgerald urged the producer to move away from the flowery language of the script Selznick had cobbled together with Oliver Garrett.

Of the scene in the library where Scarlett declares her love for Ashley, Fitzgerald wrote on January 10: "I think that in his long speech which includes the line 'passionately—with every fiber of my being,' Ashley goes entirely out of character and completely wrecks the meaning and the spirit of it all. The entire sympathy for Ashley would be lost in that moment. A man who turns down a woman is always suspected as being a prig. For an unmarried man to turn down a woman whom he loves 'passionately and with every fiber of his being' makes him simply unforgivable, inexplicable and heartless. Margaret Mitchell by having Ashley show admirable control has established a credible situation. Ashley has never allowed himself to love Scarlett 'passionately and with every fiber of his being.' That is the whole point of the scene."

"I believe you are unnecessarily worried about Melanie," Fitzgerald wrote on January 18.

"We have seen actors and actresses created by one or two strong scenes in the end of a picture, and dozens fading out in padded, hollow parts . . . how it bores the audience when they have empty things to say.

"Melanie will develop in her strong scenes—the murder of the soldier, etc.—will develop better if we haven't made her a shadowy, goody-goody with speeches that are little more than Maureen O'Sullivan 'Oh's' and 'Ah's' no matter how many words they contain. I would rather see her out of scene than annoying us by delaying action—the audience will detest her for that."

In the 1920s Fitzgerald and Sidney Howard—the great young novelist from the Midwest and the great young playright from California—had been friends in New York. But what Howard could do almost effortlessly, Fitzgerald never mastered. Fitzgerald was fired from *Gone With the Wind* on January 24, supposedly because he couldn't think of funny dialogue for Aunt Pittypat.

As an aftermath, Fitzgerald wrote to Maxwell Perkins, his editor at Scribners, that he had been "absolutely forbidden to use any words except those of Margaret Mitchell, that is, when new phrases had to be invented one had to thumb through as if it were Scripture and check out phrases of hers which would cover the situation!" But he had discovered that Mitchell's words weren't bad. As he wrote to his daughter, Scottie, *Gone With the Wind* was "not very original . . . but on the other hand it is interesting, surprisingly honest, consistent and workmanlike throughout, and I felt no contempt for it, but only a certain pity for those who consider it the supreme achievement of the human mind."

One by one the writers of January melted away, having done little to the script except rearrange dialogue. On January 25, the day before the picture started shooting, Selznick apologized to Jock Whitney for the unfinished script. "Don't get panicky at the seemingly small amount of final revised script," Selznick wrote. "There are great big gobs that will be transferred from either the Howard script or the Howard-Garrett script. . . . The important thing to remember is that the creative work that remains to be done is not of the type that leads to trouble. We have everything that we need in the book and in the Howard and Howard-Garrett scripts. The job that remains to be done is to telescope the three into the shortest possible form."

Despite Selznick's optimism, the unfinished script did cause a great deal of trouble. It also played a part in the firing of George Cukor. A number of reasons have been given for Selznick's decision to fire Cukor on February 13: the director was too slow; he was concentrating his attention on Vivien Leigh and Olivia de Havilland; Clark Gable was uncomfortable with him; he was making the movie a smaller, more intimate film than Selznick envisioned; and his use of color was subtle and did not have the vividness that Selznick had admired in Warner Bros.' *Adventures of Robin Hood*. Cukor's own explanation, given to Margaret Mitchell's friend, Susan Myrick, the day after he was fired ,was that he knew he was a good director and had good actors but, when he looked at the rushes, he saw failure.

In a letter to Mitchell, Myrick said that Cukor had become convinced that the trouble was the script. "And George has continuously taken script from day to day, compared the Garrett-Selznick version with the Howard, groaned and tried to change some parts back to the Howard script. But he seldom could do much with the scene. . . . So George just told David he would not work any longer if the script was not better and he wanted the Howard script back. David told George he was a director—not an author and he (David) was the producer and the judge of what is a good script."

There is certainly some truth in that version, although Cukor's implication that he chose to quit skirted the truth. Cukor and Selznick had been squabbling over the script since the pro-

George Cukor (left) directed scores of movies, including, memorably, The Philadelphia Story, Gaslight, Born Yesterday, Adam's Rib, *and* My Fair Lady, *for which he won an Oscar in 1964. For Selznick, Cukor made* What Price Hollywood, Little Women, A Bill of Divorcement, Dinner at Eight, *and* David Copperfield. *He discovered Katharine Hepburn and directed her in eight films. Neither Cukor's taste nor his friendship with Selznick kept Selznick (right) from firing him from* Gone With the Wind.

ducer saw the rushes from the first few days of shooting. To make the scene in Scarlett's bedroom on the morning of the barbecue work, for example, Cukor had added some dialogue with Scarlett refusing to eat and Mammy saying, "Oh, yas'm, you'se is, you gwine eat every mouthful." Even though the dialogue had come directly from the book, Selznick was angry that Cukor had dared to change the script.

As soon as he fired Cukor, Selznick called director King Vidor. "David wanted me to read all the *Gone With the Wind* scripts," said Vidor. "I picked up the stuff on Friday, and I spent the whole weekend reading it." Selznick intended to start shooting again in a week. Before Vidor was able to tell Selznick that it would take him months to put the script in order, Selznick had pressured M-G-M to pull Victor Fleming off *The Wizard of Oz*, and he coaxed Vidor into taking over that movie. Vidor was so relieved not to have to face *Gone With the Wind* that he agreed.

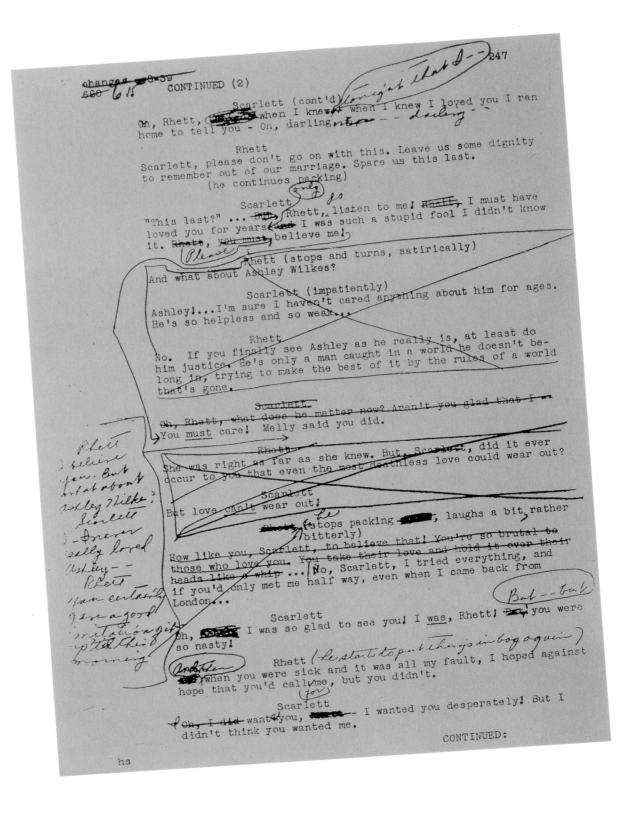

The script was revised almost daily during May and June of 1939. This revision of the scene in which Rhett leaves Scarlett was written on June 8, nearly five months after Gone With the Wind *started production and less than three weeks before filming ended.*

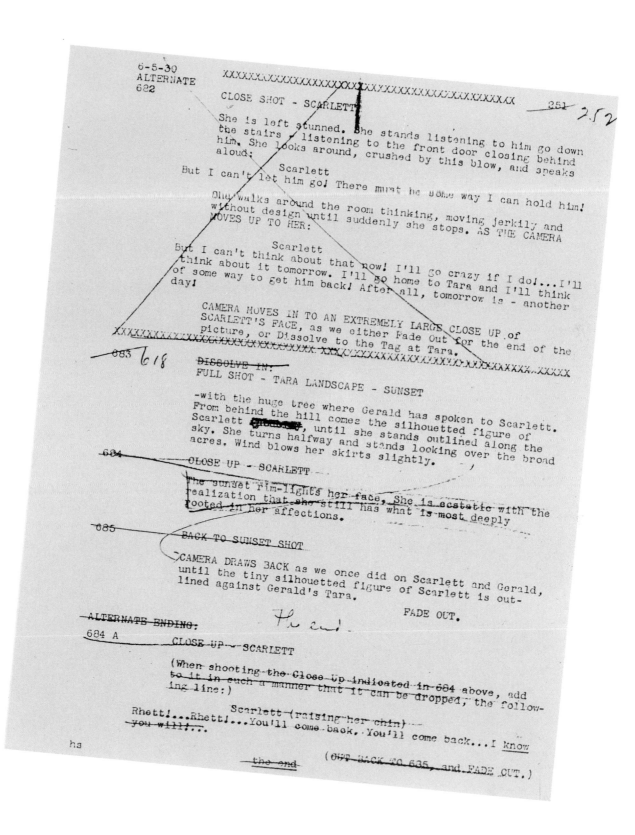

6-5-39
ALTERNATE
682

251 252

CLOSE SHOT - SCARLETT

She is left stunned. She stands listening to him go down the stairs, listening to the front door closing behind him. She looks around, crushed by this blow, and speaks aloud:

Scarlett
But I can't let him go! There must be some way I can hold him!

She walks around the room thinking, moving jerkily and without design until suddenly she stops. AS THE CAMERA MOVES UP TO HER:

Scarlett
But I can't think about that now! I'll go crazy if I do!...I'll think about it tomorrow. I'll go home to Tara and I'll think of some way to get him back! After all, tomorrow is - another day!

CAMERA MOVES IN TO AN EXTREMELY LARGE CLOSE UP of SCARLETT'S FACE, as we either Fade Out for the end of the picture, or Dissolve to the Tag at Tara.

683 618   DISSOLVE IN:
FULL SHOT - TARA LANDSCAPE - SUNSET

-with the huge tree where Gerald has spoken to Scarlett. From behind the hill comes the silhouetted figure of Scarlett   , until she stands outlined along the sky. She turns halfway and stands looking over the broad acres. Wind blows her skirts slightly.

684   CLOSE UP - SCARLETT

The sunset rim-lights her face. She is ecstatic with the realization that she still has what is most deeply rooted in her affections.

685   BACK TO SUNSET SHOT

CAMERA DRAWS BACK as we once did on Scarlett and Gerald, until the tiny silhouetted figure of Scarlett is outlined against Gerald's Tara.

FADE OUT.

ALTERNATE ENDING:

684 A   CLOSE UP - SCARLETT

(When shooting the Close Up indicated in 684 above, add to it in such a manner that it can be dropped, the following line:)

Scarlett (raising her chin)
Rhett!...Rhett!...You'll come back. You'll come back...I know you will!...

hs

the end   (CUT BACK TO 685, and FADE OUT.)

Selznick toyed with the idea of putting a happy ending on Gone With the Wind. *In one alternate ending, the last line of the movie has Scarlett saying: "Rhett! . . . Rhett! . . . You'll come back. You'll come back . . . I know you will."*

51

Fleming responded to the Garrett-Selznick script exactly as Cukor and Vidor had, although in less polite language. "David," he said, "you haven't got a fucking script."

So Fleming and Selznick went to Palm Springs with screenwriter John Lee Mahin. (As he had demonstrated with his flight to Bermuda with Jo Swerling, Selznick could only discipline himself to concentrate on one thing by walling himself off from everything else.) Mahin had written four Fleming movies, including *Red Dust* and *Captains Courageous*. Fleming and Mahin were motorcycle and drinking buddies, and the director trusted Mahin who had just done some tinkering on *The Wizard of Oz* as the last of ten writers. In Palm Springs, Mahin told Selznick to go back to Sidney Howard's script.

David didn't want to hear that advice, so he paid Mahin a thousand dollars, fired him, and borrowed screenwriter Ben Hecht from M-G-M for a week. As Hecht begins the story in his autobiography, *A Child of the Century*, "Selznick and Vic Fleming appeared at my bedside one Sunday morning at dawn. . . . " and offered him $15,000 for a week's work. Since Hecht had never read *Gone With the Wind*, David recited the book to him in such detail that it took an hour. Hecht's first response was to doubt that anyone could make a coherent movie out of such a complicated plot and so many characters. His second was to insist that one of David's many writers must have come up with a workable plot. "David suddenly remembered the first 'treatment,' discarded three years before," Hecht wrote. Selznick unearthed a copy of Sidney Howard's treatment and read it aloud. Says Hecht, "We listened to a precise and telling narrative of *Gone With the Wind*."

According to Hecht, he worked eighteen hours a day for seven days and, following Howard's treatment, completed the first nine reels of the movie. During that week, Selznick refused to let him eat anything except salted peanuts and bananas, and the stress caused a blood vessel to break in Fleming's eye.

It is always hard to know what to believe in a Ben Hecht tale. He was, after all, a writer of fiction. Studio records show that he was paid $5,000 for his week's work, not $15,000. Selznick gave him credit for restructuring the hospital sequence with Scarlett, Melanie, and wounded Confederate soldiers. But Selznick also soon brought back Sidney Howard.

Hecht had hacked away the underbrush of subplots and minor characters that had grown over Howard's original script, and, with the movie in production, there was no way Selznick could put the undergrowth back. Howard was surprised to discover that his original script was now pretty much intact. "They have done nothing much to my script except put in a lot of unnecessary movie construction in the matter of connecting scenes which has required them to cut down the good playing scenes of the book," Howard wrote his wife on April 5. That same letter began, "Darling: Here we are at the old game of waiting for Selznick. Appointment nine:thirty. No sign of same at eleven:thirty."

Howard had reluctantly agreed to give Selznick two weeks. More reluctantly, he stayed a month. Finally devoting all his energy to his now $4 million movie, Selznick sent Howard five, eight, or ten pages of single-spaced notes almost daily between April 6 and May 3 when Howard officially left *Gone With the Wind* for the last time. At least once during that time the screenwriter fled from the blizzard. Selznick pursued him with a plaintive five-page letter that began: "Dear Sidney: I tried to get you a couple of minutes after you left the studio, and left word at your hotel for you to call me, but somehow we missed connections. The contents of this note are vitally important to the shooting schedule and I should appreciate it if you will read it immediately and carefully. I am sending one copy to your hotel and one copy to your office so that you will get it without delay."

Prone to depression, Howard was dragged under by the relentless work and endless hours and by the despair that is the evening meal of writers in Hollywood. The daily letters home were his lifeline. "Less than ever do I understand this place," he wrote on April 12. "Why do they want me, why do they pay me these vast sums of money? What I have to give to one of their screen plays is something which, very evidently, they don't want. *The Light That Failed* is being re-written by a hack named Carson. *The Unvanquished* is being re-written by a punk quelquonque. I give Selznick a scene to shoot on which I work with care. I see it on the screen and he has rewritten every trace of dramatic style out of it, every bit of character and, to my mind, every bit of illusion. . . .

"Mornings like this—and there have been many of them this past eighteen months—I make up my mind to sell Tyringham, to go back to the scale on which I was living fifteen years ago. To forget about what fun cows and fields are. . . . I owe Dorman $2,600 that I can't pay. I have an enormous income tax that I can't pay. If I earn the money to pay them I have to earn the money to pay at least the tax over again next year. . . . We didn't owe a dime four years ago in Princeton. The Platt job on the house began it. Buying the farm finished it. I am now wondering seriously if I can ever get out of debt again."

In another letter to his wife, on April 8, Howard was more cynical than turned out to be necessary. "After I am gone," he wrote, Selznick "will put still another writer on my new script which he will not have read and the new man will spend another two weeks re-doing what has been done so often."

There was no other writer—except Selznick himself. And, although Selznick made a torrent of dialogue changes in May and June, he did not make major alterations in the movie's structure.

Just as Selznick was at his best in the editing room where he could see and repair flaws in the fabric of his films, he had been at his best as a writer in his final collaboration with Howard. In addition to the ending, Selznick had honed the emphasis on Tara. One of his notes reads: "We have done nothing about reintroducing the Tara note and hitting it fairly hard if we are going to create an ending in which Scarlett, bereft of her two men, is left with the thing which perhaps she loves best of all—as Gerald once told her she would, and as Ashley has told her she does—Tara. Actually I think we need something more than we have yet devised to sell her love of Tara after her marriage to Rhett. I think it even possible that one of the honeymoon dissolves could take the couple to Tara, and that in a few lines we could sell Scarlett's love of it and Rhett's promise that some day they'll spend time there. In fact, we might have Rhett make an additional gesture—one that would mean more to her than his showering her with luxuries—if he volunteered to fix the place up and restore it to its former glory." To its benefit, the movie includes all of those ideas.

Sidney Howard won an Academy Award for his screenplay of *Gone With the Wind*, but he never received the award or even saw the finished movie. In August 1939, while he was repairing a tractor on his farm, the machine—which he had left in gear—lurched forward and crushed him. He was forty-eight years old.

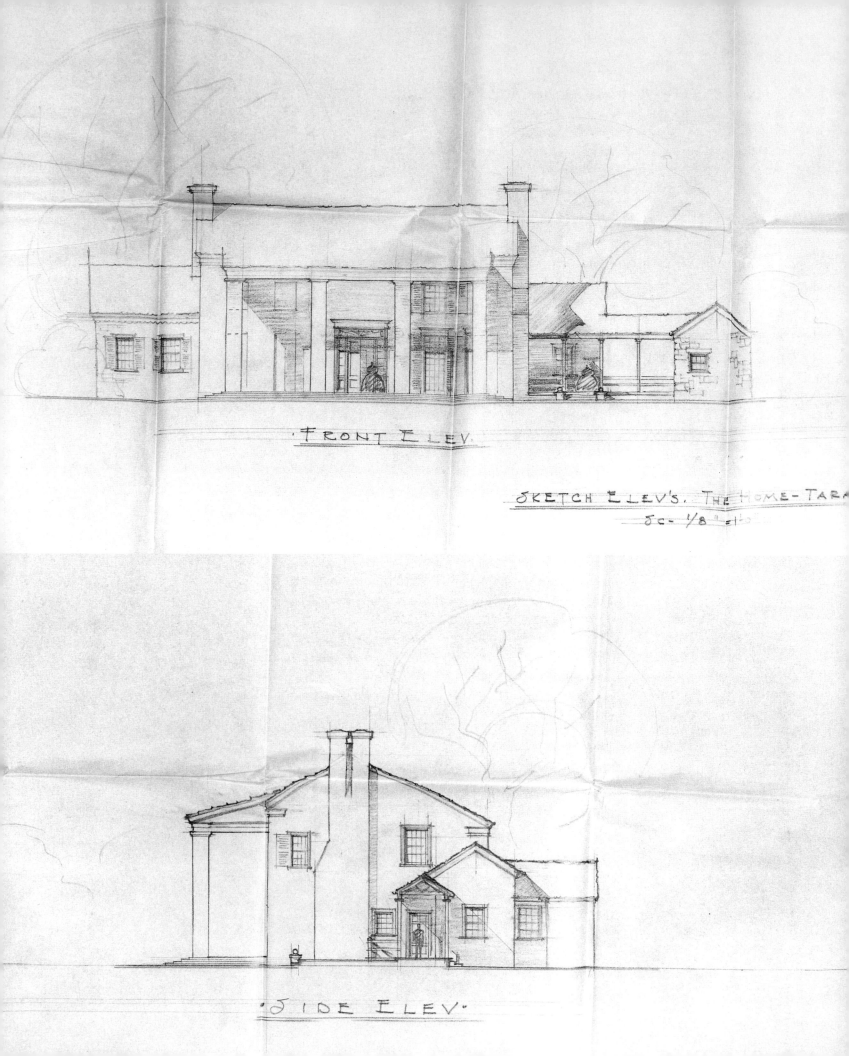

·FRONT ELEV·

SKETCH ELEV'S. THE HOME-TARA
Sc- 1/8"=1'0"

·SIDE ELEV·

TARA

From the beginning, Margaret Mitchell's Tara and David O. Selznick's Tara collided. The O'Hara plantation in northern Georgia was *Gone With the Wind*'s most potent symbol. As another classic 1939 movie demonstrated, "There's no place like home," and Scarlett didn't need ruby slippers to find her way back to Tara whenever she was in trouble.

Tara was where *Gone With the Wind* began and where it ended. "I don't want Tara," sixteen-year-old Scarlett O'Hara tells her father on page 9 of the final shooting script. "Plantations don't mean anything . . . "

> "Gerald (stops in his tracks, indignant)
> Do you mean to tell me, Katie Scarlett O'Hara, that Tara—that land doesn't mean anything to you?
>
> PROLONGED PANNING SHOT OF THE RICH, BEAUTIFUL LAND OF TARA FROM THEIR VIEW-POINT
>
> Gerald's voice (continued)
> Why, land is the only thing in this world worth working for, worth fighting for, worth dying for—because it's the only thing that lasts."

The scene ends with "the tiny, silhouetted figures of Gerald O'Hara and his daughter gazing over the lands of Tara, beautiful in the sunset, to the thematic musical accompaniment which we will use for Tara throughout the picture."

Wilbur Kurtz, the Atlanta artist and history buff who would get screen credit as *Gone With the Wind*'s historian, had a telling moment with Selznick in 1938. Kurtz said that Ashley Wilkes had come home on leave the Christmas before the battle of Gettysburg. Selznick was sure Ashley had come home the Christmas after Gettysburg.

"I insisted I was right," Kurtz wrote in a letter to his wife. "And he countered with a bet of 10 cents! I took him up and he fanned the pages of GWTW until he found the proof that he

Facing page: An architectural rendering of Tara, showing the front and side elevations. Above: The horse, groom, and elegantly dressed man and woman are not characters in the film, merely figures drawn by William Cameron Menzies to demonstrate scale.

was right. I was weakening before he turned to the marked page—but he was getting so much fun out of it, I wouldn't have backed down for ten times the amount. Triumphant, he said I owed him a dime—and when I handed it to him I asked him what on earth he was going to do with it! 'No one can ever accuse me of not reading the book!' he declared."

Selznick would make sure that all the details were accurate. He would insist that Vivien Leigh, Clark Gable, Olivia de Havilland and more than fifty other actors speak dialogue taken directly from the pages of *Gone With the Wind* rather than words strung together by the movie's many screenwriters. Tara's cotton fields would be plowed in the curved rows used in North Georgia to keep the rich soil from washing into the river bottoms. Apologies would be sent to Miss Mitchell, who had dressed Scarlett almost exclusively in green, for the necessity of adding other colors to the heroine's wardrobe. (Miss Mitchell cheerfully replied that she hadn't been aware she had dressed Scarlett so often in green but assumed it was because green was her favorite color.)

The rooms of Tara would be filled with props copied from the pages of the book—"pine knot torches for illumination," "long spills to light individual candlesticks"—and Gerald O'Hara would ride into view on "a large, white jumper."

Weeks would be spent trying to find or create some dirt, dust, or pulverized gravel to mimic the red earth of Clayton County, Georgia, where Margaret Mitchell's imagination had placed Tara. Kurtz wrote in his diary for February 5, 1938, that he and William Cameron Menzies had driven to Redlands where the earth was indeed red but, disappointingly, there were no trees. Menzies, who would be responsible for the look of *Gone With the Wind*, had already made hundreds of watercolor sketches. When he returned to Atlanta later that month, Kurtz collected dirt from a street corner and sent it to Menzies in a sardine can. The problem of the plantation's red earth would be solved a year later by grinding up red drainage tile and sending truckloads to the studio.

Margaret Mitchell refused a dozen offers from Selznick to involve herself in the transformation of her novel into a film. In response to a long questionnaire from the movie's assistant director, Eric Stacey—"At the barbecue at Twelve Oaks, how many children did Miss Mitchell visualize? Proportion of adults and children? Proportion of old and young? Were colored children and white children playing together? How many barbecue pits?"—she answered two or three of the questions but pointedly refused to describe how to tie Mammy's head rag. However, Mitchell was hardly uninterested in what "The Selznickers," as she called them, were doing to her book. She made sure that Selznick hired her friend Susan Myrick to teach the actors a Georgia accent and to watch over the movie's accuracy. And it was at her urging that the studio chose Wilbur Kurtz as technical adviser.

Kurtz and Myrick, who were aware of their roles as Mitchell's surrogates and who tended to write long, candid letters home, had considerable effect on the details of the movie. Myrick's "Script Suggestions Pages 1 thru 44" included:

```
Page 16      "Scarlett, leaving the room, takes a dish of olives
Scene 36     with her."
```

```
I never saw an olive until I was about fourteen years old. On a Georgia
plantation of the sixties, every thing to eat that could be grown on the
place was plentiful but strange or imported foods were unusual. I, there-
fore, suggest that Scarlett take with her as more typical of Georgia two
or three beaten biscuits.
```

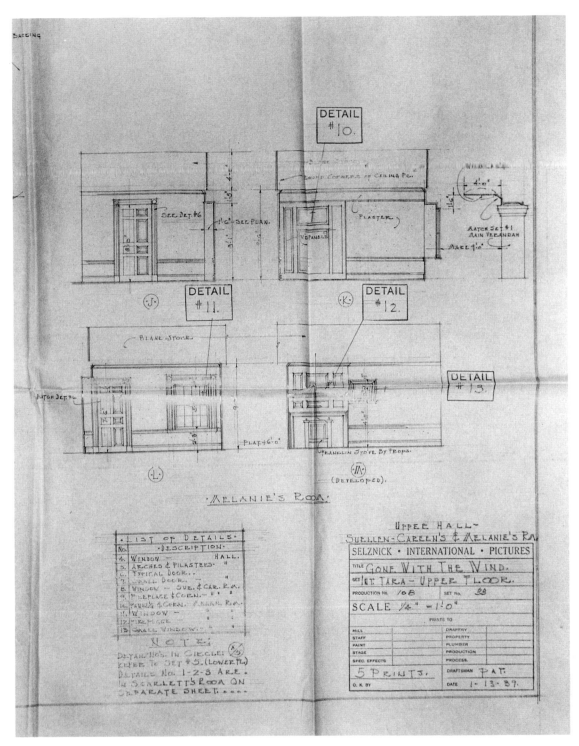

Construction drawings like the one above were the actual guides used to build Gone With the Wind's *elaborate sets. This plan of the upper floor at Tara is labeled "Suellen — Carreen's & Melanie's Room," Set No. 33, and was drawn on a scale of a quarter inch to a foot. Note the Franklin stove to be supplied by the property department.*

"GERALD'S VOICE (continued) — And to anyone with a drop of Irish blood in them, why the land they live on is like their mother. Oh, but there, there now, you're just a child. It will come to you, this love of the land. There's no getting away from it if you're Irish."

Gone With the Wind *screenplay*

Myrick's colored girls fanning the white gentry was a telling touch, and Kurtz argued Selznick out of having Scarlett shoe a horse to show the hardships faced by southern women during Reconstruction. He gave Selznick a lesson in the shaping and fitting of "white hot" horseshoes on an unwilling fifteen-hundred-pound animal and suggested that Scarlett make soap—a slave task—instead.

With Tara, the collision between Mitchell's book and Selznick's movie was not in the details. It was the concepts that could not be reconciled. Margaret Mitchell's Tara was an ugly and sprawling house constructed without help of architect by a rough Irishman. Built of white-washed brick, Tara was comfortable, but it was by no means the best looking house in Clayton County; and even the best North Georgia houses had none of the elegance of homes in Savannah.

But David Selznick could no more resist grandness on the screen than he could resist grand gestures in roulette, where he always bet on too many numbers at a time. David was a roman-

These early renderings of Tara have slender wooden columns and a definite twentieth-century feel. The house in the film has square whitewashed brick columns and a more solid look. "No one will be entirely pleased with Tara," Wilbur Kurtz wrote in his journal. "Every reader of the book has seen it his own way." Kurtz, an accomplished watercolorist, drew numerous sketches of Tara.

tic, and his Tara—bathed in the splendor of an artificial sunset created by the studio's special effects department—had nothing of crude realism. It was a graceful, white columned, romantic house.

Lecturing to Selznick on rural architecture in Clayton County, Kurtz told the man he called "the Boss" that there was "nothing gorgeous at Tara." Selznick responded that moviegoers from Atlanta would not be a large percentage of the movie's audience. Maybe Selznick was right, Kurtz thought, and other moviegoers needed to see the South as they had imagined it. "Maybe a true representation, falling short of what would be expected, would be laid up to sloven or inefficient workmanship."

Selznick was undoubtedly right, since Tara and the neighboring Wilkes plantation Twelve Oaks—as metaphors of the graceful life the South would lose—needed to be worthy of mourning. So Selznick inflated Mitchell's Tara, and he turned the interior of the stately Twelve Oaks into a palace which Myrick had fun ridiculing for the benefit of the book's author. Mitchell had described Twelve Oaks as a white house of "perfect symmetry . . . tall of columns, wide of verandas, flat of roof, beautiful as a woman is beautiful who is so sure of her charm that she can be generous and gracious to all."

"I swear these fools are spending enough to make ten movies," Myrick wrote to Mitchell during the shooting of the barbecue scenes. "The castle they have built for Twelve Oaks. . . . There were 250 extras at the outdoor shots we made in Busch Gardens in Pasadena (incidentally the barbecue setting looked like the palace at Versailles) not including the twenty colored waiters and cooks, the ten maid servants and five Mammys and ten little nigger chillun and fifteen white chillun!" As to the halls and staircases of Twelve Oaks, Myrick said she "almost died at the magnificence of the place. Looks like Grand Central Station or the Palace at Potsdam."

Faithful in details of pine knot torches and embroidery, in red horses for the Tarleton boys and Jersey cows in Tara's fields because Holsteins were unknown in the South in 1860, Selznick could not force himself to be faithful in tone. Yet even Margaret Mitchell recognized the strength of Selznick's myth. As she wrote in a letter two years after *Gone With the Wind* was released, "I believe that we southerners could write the truth about the ante-bellum South, its few slaveholders, its yeomen farmers, its rambling, comfortable houses just fifty years away from log cabins, until Gabriel blows his trump—and everyone would go on believing in the Hollywood version. The sad part is that many southerners believe this myth even more ardently than northerners."

In the same letter, Mitchell spoke of nearly bursting into laughter at the sight of Twelve Oaks, whose magnificence, she said, was rivaled only by the state capitol in Montgomery, Alabama. In that case, she was laughing at an illusion. The exterior of Twelve Oaks was never built.

The Corinthian columns in the hall, the elegant double staircase, the bedroom where the girls nap in fourposter beds, and the library with its huge globe of the world filled Stages 11 and 12, but the house was created by a process that was called at various studios a trick shot, a matte shot, or a glass shot. It was simply—although more difficult than it sounds—a painting that was then photographed. At Selznick International, Jack Cosgrove, the head of the special effects department, painted on glass. At M-G-M the same year, the Emerald City and Witch's Castle in *The Wizard of Oz* were four-foot-wide oil pastel drawings on black cardboard.

Tara, although it lacked much of its roof, was as real as any studio creation. It was the facade of a house, full height with imposing square columns. ("If I'm gonna take a bow on anything I did about this picture, it would be that I kept round columns off of Tara," Kurtz told an Atlanta audience twenty-three years later.) Selznick turned down at least twenty different renderings of Tara before he saw a sketch he liked. It has been said that the drawing Selznick approved was the first sketch he had turned down—resubmitted by Menzies months later when the start of production was so close that Selznick was forced to make up his mind.

It was not really that Selznick did not know what he wanted; but the picture in his head was sometimes too indistinct to be put into words. He had the first scene of the movie—Scarlett being courted on the porch of Tara by the Tarleton boys—shot and reshot before he realized that what was bothering him about the scene was the dress Scarlett was wearing. The "green flowered muslin" had been described on Page 1 of the book, and Walter Plunkett, the costume designer, followed the Selznick rules of design: "Do not vary anything from the book. The book is law; the book is the Bible." Months later, Selznick would realize that he wanted to dress Scarlett in white, so she would appear as youthful and virginal as possible in this last innocent moment before the war. (The supremacy of the producer on *Gone With the Wind* is demonstrated in the daily production logs. Director George Cukor shot that scene on January 26. Selznick had it reshot in March by Victor Fleming, in June with Scarlett in a white dress, and in October once again.)

Like most movie houses, Tara, which was built on the studio back lot called the Forty Acres, was a hollow shell. The facade cost $12,059, $2,809 more than the original estimate. Scarlett's bedroom and the parlor where the O'Hara family said evening prayers were constructed on Stage 3.

The entry hall at Tara was sketched by Dorothea Holt, who had studied fine arts and architecture at the University of Southern California and then studied for two years at Art Center (Collection Dennis A. Shaw and James Tumblin). During the nineteen thirties, as the Depression forced architects out of business, most young architecture graduates drifted into the studios as sketch artists. Holt worked in the studios for fifteen years and then went to Walt Disney's WED, where she was involved in planning and sketching New Orleans Square for Disneyland.

Selznick, whose second guessing usually involved grander or more expensive ideas, sent a memo to Menzies and the art director Lyle Wheeler on March 21, when the movie had been shooting for two months: "I am sure that you both share my regret that we didn't go further on the size and beauty on the interior of Tara. In this connection, if we should ever do any retakes of either the Prayer Scene or the Wedding Scene (the latter is a particularly strong possibility because of the wretched photography), I think we ought to try to so design the shots as to get more feeling of beauty and elegance into these rooms. . . . I am aware that our sets are a little exaggerated in size even now—but I am convinced that for theatrical purposes we should have gone further. This makes all the more necessary getting a real feeling of gorgeous countryside and extensive acreage around Tara."

That "gorgeous countryside and extensive acreage" was a perfect movie blend of the real and the artificial. The giant oaks in front of Tara were telephone poles to which wood ribs were attached to create a thick artificial tree trunk. Chicken wire was nailed to the ribs, and the whole

Another version of the entry hall by Dorothea Holt has more ele-gant furnishings. Selznick insisted that Tara be much grander than the house that Margaret Mitchell created. "We had to go out and sketch furniture the set decorator, Joseph Platt, found in antique stores," Holt says. "And then bring the sketches back and put them in the sets. For Tara, the studio rented one highboy worth $2,400."

The tag in the upper right hand corner of this drawing by "Mac" Johnson, which may show the O'Hara family at evening prayers, identifies it as Set No. 5, interior of the living room at Tara, but Holt says it is actually the O'Hara's dining room. Before she married the Irish immigrant Gerald O'Hara and moved to the rough country of North Georgia, Ellen Robillard was the daughter of one of the wealthiest and proudest families of Savannah. Her quiet good taste is in contrast to the gaudiness of Scarlett's house in postwar Atlanta.

MAC JOHNSON.

A different drawing of Set No. 5 shows how much the conception of a room could change. A memo from Selznick to his production designer, William Cameron Menzies, and his art director, Lyle Wheeler, on March 21, 1939, began: "I am sure that you both share my regret that we didn't go further on the size and beauty of the interior of Tara." As to the living room, "nothing much would have to be done with it except to so light and photograph and dress it as to get a real feeling of luxury and wealth."

thing was plastered, imprinted with impressions from real bark, and painted. Real tree branches were tied to each trunk, and clusters of leaves were wired on to cast the proper shadows on the facade of the house.

The house was also framed by genuine trees, including two full-grown magnolias purchased by the studio. Newly planted shrubs and vines mimicked Georgia plants and were enhanced with fabric blossoms created by the property department. Elsewhere on the Forty Acres a stand of cottonwoods and two gnarled sycamores served as background to Gerald O'Hara's ride from Twelve Oaks at the beginning of the movie.

In April, Menzies went to Chico in Northern California to shoot the sunsets that would be required for Scarlett's walk home with her father. It was an exercise in futility. "Standing by for clouds," is repeated again and again on the daily production records. Followed by "bad light."

Selznick was always obsessed by detail—a man finding his way through the forest by touching every tree; on *Gone With the Wind*, which he saw as the most important movie anyone had ever made, not only Tara but everything inside it must be the biggest and the best. After her first wardrobe fittings for her role as Carreen, Scarlett's youngest sister, Ann Rutherford was dismayed. "They brought a bootmaker out from New York who did the most enchanting shoes with two or three different types of leather," she says. "And there were petticoats with all this beautiful eyelet ruffling and lace and ribbons tied in little bows. And each petticoat was prettier than the last. I was enchanted but horrified. I had done Gene Autry westerns, and I was well aware you put on Mary Jane pumps because the shoes didn't show and nobody ever saw your underwear. I have no idea what caused me to have the temerity to suggest that I might save Selznick some money, but I said, 'Oh, Mr. Selznick, I think you're spending far too much money on our underwear.' And he said, 'Ann, your father is the richest plantation owner in Georgia, and I want you to feel like a rich plantation owner's daughter.'"

It is probably no accident that Selznick's Tara looked remarkably like the two-story colonial mansion that was the headquarters and logo of Selznick International Pictures. And it is certainly no accident that the make-believe plantation could never quite live up to Selznick's romantic view of it. David was a rich plantation owner's son, or at least the son of a mogul ruined by the Hollywood wars. He was his father's favorite, and his father was—briefly, at least—the World Film Corporation. By the time he was fourteen, David was an employee of and heir to Lewis J. Selznick Pictures. Lewis taught his youngest son to live high and spend wide and never worry about tomorrow; and he bathed him in money and optimism even on the edge of bankruptcy.

If David was a Hollywood prince, disinherited by his father's failure, Irene—daughter of M-G-M's Louis B. Mayer—was the most royal of Hollywood princesses. But they were Jewish royalty, and the white mansion with green shutters that David created as his logo and his temple was something else. It sat a mile or so east of M-G-M, and was the studio built by the silent film producer/director Thomas Ince. The first time Irene was allowed to go out alone with David, he had pointed to the graceful building and told her that was the studio he would like to have. He was twenty-four years old and would soon be fired from M-G-M for arrogance. Seven years later, Eastern wealth and gentile aristocracy—Jock Whitney's friendship and Jock and Cornelius Vanderbilt "Sonny" Whitney's money—would buy it for him, although he could inhabit it only in his imagination—and on the screen.

Whitney and his sister, Joan, had inherited much of their father's $179 million estate, and Jock was enamored of racehorses and the movie business. During the Roaring Twenties, the rich had become intrigued with the new Hollywood glamour; Jock, who liked to date actresses, was no exception. And Selznick—like many of the men who shaped America's fantasies—yearned for wealth and aristocracy. "David just wanted to be Jock Whitney—his money, his style, his entree," Joseph Mankiewicz observed. Selznick—second generation Hollywood—was charming and literate. The friendship between Whitney and Selznick was real and immediate and never quite believed by Whitney's wealthy, aristocratic friends or by the other studio chiefs.

"I'd like to see a new sketch for the last scene of the picture—the pull back," Selznick wrote Menzies and Jack Cosgrove on June 5, three weeks before the picture finished shooting. "To see just how much we can get into it of long acres of cotton fields and a sense of Tara fully prosperous as we've never seen it in the picture, all of which I should think Jack might do in his painting. Perhaps I should not say 'as we've never seen it in the picture,' for perhaps we should see something very close to it in the pullback that is going to be made on the same location in connection with Gerald and Scarlett's walk."

It was Menzies who made concrete what David imagined and gave *Gone With the Wind* a visual coherence despite the fact that the scenes in the movie were shot by four different directors. Afterward—in eight pages of pencilled notes now tucked into the corner of a box in the Selznick Archive—Menzies described his use of color and composition and the emotional effects they could provide.

"In the sequence between Scarlett & O'Hara walking up to and stopping in front of Tara," he wrote of the beginning of the movie and the pull-back shot which showed Tara in all its magnificence against a sunset sky, "there's the almost imperceptible darkening and enriching of the Values and color until we achieve the violent contrast of the pull-back shot. Cosgrove painted the distance in what is called close values and cool colors which against the violent blacks of the tree and the silhouetted figures gave a very convincing effect of depth and distance. Also in the colors & in the printing the whole effect through the walk became cooler & darker, giving the effect of approaching night. The achievement was in going from a rather idyllic family light scene & blending without shock into a very strong dramatic effect to point up O'Hara's lines."

And where *Gone With the Wind* began, at Tara, it ended. To the background music of "Tara's Theme," Scarlett—no longer sixteen in a white dress, but a dozen years older, widowed twice, with a husband who has just left her and only Tara as her shield—stands on the hill where she once stood with her father and understands fully what Gerald was trying to tell her.

"FULL SHOT - TARA LANDSCAPE - SUNSET
With the huge tree where Gerald has spoken to Scarlett. From behind the hill comes the silhouetted figure of Scarlett until she stands outlined along the sky. She turns halfway and stands looking over the broad acres. Wind blows her skirts slightly."

That stage direction is a puzzlement. "Wind blows her skirts slightly." Is it the wind of change? And, if so, does it bring loss or renewal? Is it the wind that swept the Old South away and left Scarlett standing? The wind against which she is powerless or the wind that has no power against her?

The winds of change were already marshaling against David Selznick. Or, perhaps it would be more accurate to say that he was marshaling them against himself. By 1941, Selznick International Pictures would be liquidated—a victim of David's restlessness and self-aggrandizement and Jock Whitney's frustration with David's extravagance, disorganization, and inconsistency. There were tax reasons too; and, a year later, David made the worst decision of his career. Having learned nothing from Scarlett O'Hara about legacies and the things you need to hold on to, he sold his share of *Gone With the Wind* to the Whitneys.

"Wind blows her skirts slightly.

CAMERA DRAWS BACK as we once did on Scarlett and Gerald, until the tiny silhouetted figure of Scarlett is outlined against Gerald's Tara.

                                                        FADE OUT"

The silhouettes of Scarlett at the ends of Part I and Part II are among the most enduring images in the film. (Two scenes from Gone With the Wind © *1939 Turner Entertainment Co. All Rights Reserved. Photo: Photofest)*

In her bedroom before the barbecue, Scarlett, wearing her mountainous
petticoats and stays, leans against the footboard of her bed as Mammy
comes through the doorway with a tray of food.
"MAMMY: Ah has tole you an' tole you dat you kin allus tell a lady
by de way dat she eats in front o' folks lak a bird! An' Ah ain't aimin' fer you
to go ter Mist' John Wilkes an' eat lak a fiel' han' an' gobble lak a hawg."
Gone With the Wind *screenplay*

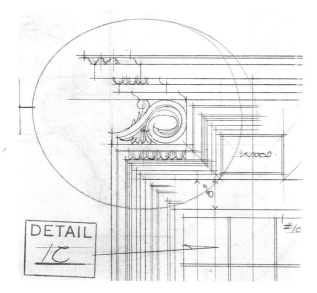

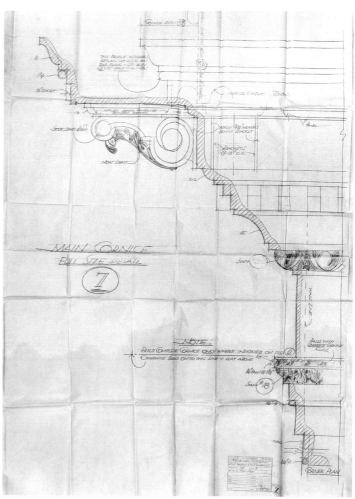

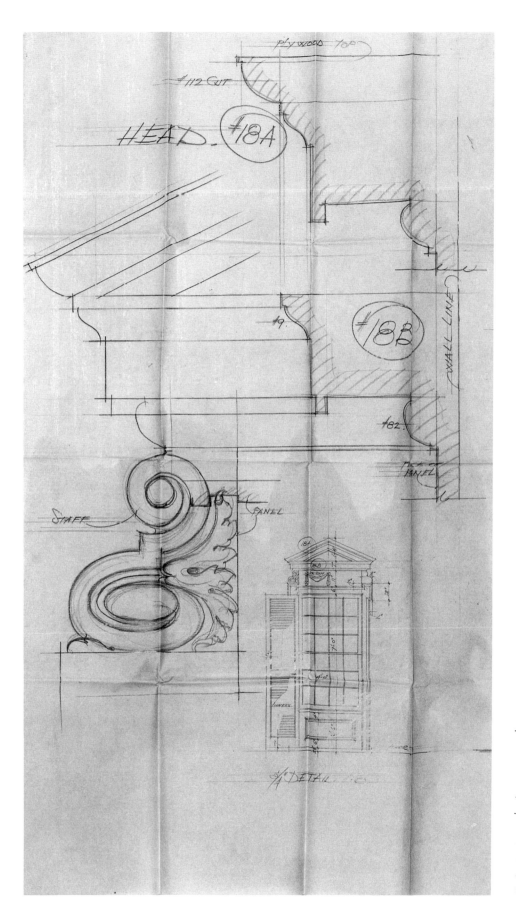

These construction drawings of cornices, door jambs, door sills, and other interior details in the rooms of Twelve Oaks give more than a hint of why Gone With the Wind was so expensive. The lower floor interiors that were built for the Wilkes plantation cost $6,043 — almost $5,000 over budget. "They bought Hobe Erwin wallpaper for Twelve Oaks for twenty-five dollars a roll, which was extremely expensive then," says Dorothea Holt. "Then they sprayed it down so you couldn't see the design. They might as well have used any old Sears wallpaper."

While the other girls are taking required afternoon naps between the barbecue and the ball, Scarlett peeks down the stairs at two men talking in the Twelve Oaks entry hall below. The rather ordinary staircase in this Dorothea Holt drawing was replaced in the movie by a curved double staircase that had been copied from a mansion in South Carolina.

A bedroom, the entry hall, and the library at Twelve Oaks. That plantation's movie magnificence disconcerted
Margaret Mitchell. "I have been embarrassed on many occasions by finding myself included among writers
who pictured the South as a land of white-columned mansions whose wealthy owners had thousands of slaves and
drank thousands of juleps," she wrote in a letter on July 23, 1942. "I have been surprised, too, for North Georgia
certainly was no such country — if it ever existed anywhere — and I took great pains to describe
North Georgia as it was. But people believe what they like to believe and the mythical Old South has too strong a
hold on their imaginations to be altered by the mere reading of a 1,037-page book."
Margaret Mitchell's Gone With the Wind Letters: 1936–1949

MAC JOHNSON

This scene rendering of the library at Twelve Oaks was drawn by Joseph McMillan "Mac" Johnson. A graduate of the University of Southern California School of Architecture, Johnson later earned several Academy Award nominations for art direction, most notably on Alfred Hitchcock's To Catch a Thief *(1955) and M-G-M's* Mutiny on the Bounty *(1962). He then moved into special visual effects and was nominated in that category for* The Greatest Story Ever Told *(1965) and* Ice Station Zebra *(1968).*

Scarlett tells Ashley of her love, while Rhett lies hidden on the couch. This version of the Twelve Oaks library, drawn by Dorothea Holt, comes closer to the room as it appeared in the movie. It even includes the striking globe of the world in the right foreground. As to the furnishings, Wilbur Kurtz was expected to advise on "the difference between the French influence superimposed upon a Clayton County rural establishment" by Ellen O'Hara at Tara "and the English traditions of Twelve Oaks."

Scarlett swore that, after the war, she would never be hungry again. This trio of scene renderings shows a prosperous Scarlett and Rhett watching the construction of their house in postwar Atlanta, a scene that did not survive in the finished film; Rhett riding with his daughter, Bonnie Blue; and a party that never took place in which a group of children, dressed as Indians, play in teepees on the Butler's huge lawn.

Most of the money Rhett made running the blockade during the war was poured into this gaudy Atlanta house. Both scene renderings share a stained-glass window, red velvet curtains, globe lamps, and a marble statue, but, architecturally and in tone, they present different pictures of the staircase and landing. (Detail for the Butlers' stained-glass window: Collection Dennis A. Shaw and James Tumblin).

"*Working on* Gone With the Wind *became a terrible drudge. We had to be in at nine in the morning, but Selznick never saw the art director until eleven o'clock at night, so they kept us doing sketches until then. We were working in watercolor, and the sketches were dripping wet when Lyle Wheeler and Bill Menzies would take them from us and go up to Selznick who might not look at them until 2:00 A.M.*" (Dorothea Holt, 1996)

"SCARLETT: *And can we still have our big new house in Atlanta?*
RHETT: *Yes. (laughing) And it can be as ornate as you want
it. Marble terraces, stained-glass windows and all.*
SCARLETT: *Oh, Rhett, won't everybody be jealous! I want
everybody who's been mean to me to be pea-green
with envy."*
Gone With the Wind *screenplay*

The furnishings for the Butler house and the movie's other houses were selected by Edward Boyle, a member of the studio's property depart-ment, and Joseph Platt, an interior design consultant for House and Garden. *Selznick, who approved every detail of the set decorations, gave Platt an "Interiors by" screen credit and Boyle the slightly inferior "Interior decoration by" credit. "We did twenty-five full-sized sketches of the stairhall in the Butler house because Selznick wanted the most frightening look for the staircase for Scarlett to fall down." (Dorothea Holt, 1996) These rejected staircases were not threatening enough.*

"Dear Bill: Lyle tonight brought me in a sketch of Rhett's bedroom
which I am sorry to have to say is shockingly bad. It is neither an
attractive set nor does it have any period flavor nor any of the character
we have discussed in connection with Rhett's house. Frankly we seem to
have been in such a mess about Rhett's house for so long that I am
extremely worried about this series of sets especially because of the
terrific pressure of time on them due to our failure to get satisfactory
conceptions and also because of the importance of this house to
the second half of the picture."
Telegram from David O. Selznick to William Menzies,
March 30, 1939

BURNING

The night David Selznick burned Atlanta and found his Scarlett O'Hara among the embers—December 10, 1938—is always recorded as the start of production on *Gone With the Wind*.

That cold California night catches the imagination. All the Technicolor cameras in the world—all seven of them—were turning while the flames leaped and bit at old sets being sacrificed for the new. Disguised as Atlanta's railroad yards and munitions warehouses, the Temple of Jerusalem from *King of Kings* and the Great Gate from *King Kong* twisted and writhed and tumbled down. The air was thick with smoke and hot with expectation. Talent agent Myron Selznick arrived late and drunk—he would drink himself to death before his forty-sixth birthday—and told his younger brother, "Hey, Genius, here's your Scarlett O'Hara," as he introduced David to Vivien Leigh.

Or so the legend goes.

Actually, the first production photography charged to *Gone With the Wind* had occurred eight months earlier. In March 1938, after a drenching twenty-four-hour rain, Clarence Slifer had been sent out to photograph clouds. Slifer filmed ten thousand feet of what he called "exceedingly beautiful cloud formations" that he thought could be used as backgrounds for the main titles that would be created in a laboratory sixteen months later.

The man who sent Slifer to film clouds was forty-two-year-old William Cameron Menzies. By that time, Menzies was already legendary as an art director. He had gotten his first movie job around 1920 by improvising palm trees in Fort Lee, New Jersey. All Menzies could find were two palm leaf fans. "I stripped them down to palms," he said, "and to secure my effect,

Facing page: On paper and on the screen, Menzies painted Scarlett and Rhett's escape from Atlanta in what he defined as "great masses of red and black" (Collection Dennis A. Shaw and James Tumblin). Above: On December 10, 1938, Selznick recreated the burning of Atlanta's munition depots seventy-four years earlier.

William Cameron Menzies (left) with Selznick and George Cukor (right). (The Fred A. Parrish Collection).
"Bill Menzies spent perhaps a year of his life in laying out camera angles, lighting effects, and other important
directorial contributions to Gone With the Wind, *a large number of which are in the picture just as he designed*
them a year before Vic Fleming came on the film," Selznick wrote in a letter to Screen Directors Guild president
Frank Capra in January 1940. "In addition, there are a large number of scenes which he personally directed,
including a most important part of the spectacle." Selznick was complaining that neither George Cukor, Sam
Wood, nor Menzies had been given sufficient credit for their directorial contributions to the movie.

stood on a chair in the sun, waving the palm leaves so that the shadow was thrown on the wall in back of the actors." He was just out of art school.

By 1928, Menzies had come west with the movies and had won the first Academy Award ever given for art direction, for *The Dove*. "Bill could take the most ordinary thing in a picture and make it cinematically fascinating," said Ted Haworth (*Strangers on a Train*), one of the legions of younger art directors Menzies influenced. "Nobody could do what he did, just nobody."

By 1938, Menzies had directed seven movies, only one of them memorable. A brilliant composer of spectacle, he was a flop when he was left on a sound stage with three actors and five pages of dialogue. The exception to his failure as a director was *Things to Come*, his stunning, Le Corbusier-influenced recreation of H. G. Wells's vision of the future.

No one ever had a bad word to say about Bill Menzies. He was a laughing Scotsman with a taste for hard liquor and the ability to hold it. His parents were Scottish immigrants, but he was taken back to Scotland by his mother when he was six. He returned to graduate from Yale and the Art Students League. The words the other craftsmen used to describe him were "kind," "generous," and "artistic genius."

Selznick, who was dazzled by Menzies' work on the cave sequence in *The Adventures of Tom Sawyer*, showed his respect by paying him $1,000 a week. And, as early as September 1937,

Selznick was inventing the screen credit he would give Menzies on *Gone With the Wind* two years later. He tried "Assistant to the Producer" but had already almost decided on "Production Designed by William Cameron Menzies" before Menzies had made a single sketch.

No movie had ever had a "Production Designed by . . ." credit. Movies had art directors who designed sets to the specifications of director and producer; and, in the late 1930s, color film was pretty much under the control of Technicolor, which rented cameramen along with their cameras. But of the thousands of decisions Selznick made on *Gone With the Wind*—which actors to cast, what costumes to approve, what sets to build, what scenes to cut—giving Menzies responsibility for the look of the film was one of the three most important; it was equaled only by the choice of Vivien Leigh and by the decision to shoot in Technicolor despite the added cost.

Those last two decisions might have been made by any shrewd producer. Using Menzies as his paintbrush was the kind of acuteness that made Selznick something more.

As usual, Selznick stumbled to his conclusions in a series of memos.

July 29, 1937: "I would like to see him [Menzies] actively take charge of the physical preparation of GONE WITH THE WIND, including advance work on the sets, handling and selection of location shots, process shots, etc; layouts and effects, etc. for the mass action scenes; investigations and suggestions leading to the proper handling of the street sets without an inordinate expense; and a dozen other things leading to proper organization of the great and troublesome physical aspects of GONE WITH THE WIND."

August 12, 1937: "I should go even further than this and have him do a complete cutting script with sketches from the first shot to the last on the entire job of GONE WITH THE WIND. . . . I feel too that he may be the answer to what I have long sought for, which is a precut picture."

September 1, 1937: "There is also the job of the montage sequences, which I plan on having Menzies not merely design and lay out but also, in large degree, actually direct. In short it is my plan to have the whole physical side of this picture . . . personally handled by one man who has little or nothing else to do—and that man, Menzies. Menzies may turn out to be one of the most valuable factors in properly producing this picture."

Menzies, art director Lyle Wheeler, and their primary staff artists J. McMillan Johnson and Dorothea Holt would create at least 1,500 sketches,[1] of which 200 remain in the Selznick Archive. Every camera angle, lighting angle, and character interaction would be sketched in color. Using the technique perfected by Walt Disney for *Snow White and the Seven Dwarfs* (1937), but which he himself had been using since *Bulldog Drummond* in 1929, Menzies would storyboard the action in the fire sequence shot by shot, creating on paper what the eye should see on screen. Then he would direct the Burning as well as most of the other moments of spectacle that did not include the major actors.

In a speech Menzies gave at the University of Southern California in 1929, just after the movies learned to talk, he said that the essential qualification for his job was "great ingenuity." In addition, he must be "a cartoonist, a costumer, a marine painter, a designer of ships, an interior decorator, a landscape painter, a dramatist, an inventor, an historical, and now, an acoustical expert" with "a knowledge of architecture of all periods and nationalities."

Despite the fact that Menzies was, to a greater or lesser degree, all of those things, his 1,500 sketches did not supply Selznick with a pre-cut film. Since the script was constantly changing,

1. Ezra Goodman, who interviewed Menzies in 1945 for an *American Cinematographer* article, said Menzies made 1,200 sketches on an ordinary film and 2,500 on *Gone With the Wind*. In his book *David O. Selznick's Hollywood*, Ronald Haver used art department records to make a guess of 1,500 drawings.

sets had to be redrawn, camera angles didn't work, and characters who were in a scene one day were positioned differently the next or were written out of the scene altogether.

The fire sequence, which shows Rhett and Scarlett fleeing Atlanta with Melanie and her newborn baby in the back of their wagon, is a perfect example. In November 1938, Menzies had written his own scenario for the fire sequence. What reached the screen was vastly different. In a Ph.D. thesis, Alan Vertrees compared the sixty-six drawings that remain in Menzies's storyboard of the fire sequence with Menzies's scenario, various subsequent scripts by different writers, and the sequence as it appears on the screen. His analysis demonstrates how few of the shots Menzies originally planned for the escape from Atlanta are in the final movie. Changes were made in every script; on the stages when Clark Gable, Butterfly McQueen, and Vivien Leigh did close-ups of action that had been photographed in long shots (using doubles) the night of December 10; and in the editing room, where Selznick and his editor Hal Kern rearranged the shots.

Every movie is a collaboration. This tritest of observations about movies is also the truest. Even if one person writes, directs, and produces, that person cannot also nail the sets together, move arc lights into position, dye the fabric for the costumes, and change the film in the camera. In a 1945 interview, Menzies defined his production designs as "an intermediate process between the printed word and its visualization on celluloid." The ultimate power on *Gone With the Wind* belonged to Selznick. What Menzies succeeded in doing was to make the movie a coherent visual whole, despite the fact that *Gone With the Wind*'s first director, George Cukor, was replaced after fourteen days by Victor Fleming, who shot for two months and then collapsed and was temporarily replaced by Sam Wood. The glue Menzies used was color, composition, and lighting.

As early as 1929 Menzies had written about the problems of designing for the screen. The designer was handicapped, he said, because the camera is "a very analytical observer" and "does not photograph as the mind sees. If, for instance, you photograph a romantic location such as a picturesque European street, you will have an accurate reproduction—minus the atmosphere, texture and color. Hence it is always better to substitute a set that is the impression of that street as the mind sees it, slightly romanticized, simplified and over-textured." The look of *Gone With the Wind* was romanticized, simplified, and multi-textured for emotional effect from the oversized rooms in the great plantation houses to the bold colors to the breathtaking pullback shot of thousands of wounded Confederate soldiers, which Menzies designed.

Menzies's own words—written after *Gone With the Wind* was finished and he was trying to translate his images into a less precise language—show how he painted with color to create emotional impact. In the Atlanta bazaar sequence, he said he had sacrificed "what might be called symphonic colors to the realistic to really make an effect of locally decorated and home-made effect. At the same time overdoing its brilliance a bit to contrast with the later drabness illustrating the disintegration of the South." The Atlanta railroad station when Ashley returned home on leave was shot "with a blue filter to throw the whole scene into a wintry cold monotone to punch up the rigours of the Southern life at this time." When Ashley returned to the front, his "grey uniform against the grey fog gave the effect of an almost absence of color. A very light blue filter helped this without really adding color." When Scarlett searched for Dr. Meade among the hundreds of wounded soldiers, even the sky was colorless "throwing the one bit of color of Scarlett's hat into prominence to give the effect of one tiny foreign figure in the massed carpet of wounded." Menzies's Oscar citation would read: "Outstanding achievement in the use of color for the enhancement of dramatic mood."

What is hard to comprehend today when any ten-year-old child can shoot a roll of 35mm color film with decent results is how difficult color film was in 1939. In the late 1920s, there had been some experiments with crude two-strip color, but audiences had found the tint ugly and unappealing. *Gone With the Wind* was only the thirteenth movie made in the new three-strip Technicolor. When the movie won an Oscar for color cinematography, it was the first time color had been recognized by the Academy, and it would be 1957, almost twenty years later, before color cinematography ceased to be a separate category.

Selznick International Pictures was a small studio. It made two or three pictures a year while M-G-M, Paramount, and Warner Bros. produced a movie every ten days. But, by 1939, SIP had a sophisticated knowledge of color without which the special effects in *Gone With the Wind* would not have been possible. Selznick International had made the second Technicolor movie, *The Garden of Allah*, in 1936, and the fifth, *A Star Is Born*, as well as *Nothing Sacred* in 1937, and *The Adventures of Tom Sawyer* in 1938. Only Warner Bros. had made as many color films before *Gone With the Wind*. In 1939, the victory of color movies was by no means assured. M-G-M, the industry titan, did not make its first color picture until midway through 1938. Universal would not release its first three-strip Technicolor movie until 1942.

SIP's expertise in color was not due to David Selznick. Although, after changing his mind several times, Selznick would eventually decide to shoot *Gone With the Wind* in color, he thought color films cost too much. Making a picture in black-and-white was more profitable. The week *Gone With the Wind* finished production, in June 1939, Selznick asked his staff to calculate how much money shooting in color had added to the cost of the movie. He was told that the tangible costs—extra cameramen, developing and printing, special lighting, etc.— amounted to $428,594.92. The intangible costs—the extra time it took to light the sets, to move the ponderous camera equipment around, and to consult with Technicolor advisors—totaled another $118,750.

The man who saw the future in color was SIP's chairman, Jock Whitney. David and Jock had tried and failed to form a company together in 1932. So, in 1933, Whitney and his cousin, Cornelius Vanderbilt "Sonny" Whitney, bought into Technicolor and founded Pioneer Pictures to make movies in color. The first three-strip Technicolor feature, *Becky Sharp* (1935), was produced by Pioneer. When Selznick International Pictures was formed in October 1935, with most of the money put up by the Whitneys and Pioneer, SIP was obligated to combine with Pioneer to make color movies.

"Before GWTW started, Selznick produced six pictures, three in color and three in black-and-white," Clarence Slifer said, looking back forty-three years later.[2] "With each color production that we made before the start of GWTW, we gained in experience, equipment, and personnel."

Slifer was assistant to Jack Cosgrove, the head of Selznick's special effects department. On *Gone With the Wind* Menzies and Cosgrove were given screen credit on the same separate card, the letters in Menzies's name two-thirds the size of Selznick's name, which, in turn, was two-thirds the size of Clark Gable's name. "This production designed by William Cameron Menzies," and just below in slightly smaller letters, "Special Photographic Effects Jack Cosgrove" stayed on the screen a full six seconds, as long as "Produced by David O. Selznick" and twice as long as "Music by Max Steiner" or "Screenplay by Sidney Howard."

2. Selznick International had made four movies in color—*The Garden of Allah*, *A Star Is Born*, *Nothing Sacred*, and *The Adventures of Tom Sawyer*—and four films in black-and-white—*Little Lord Fauntleroy*, *The Prisoner of Zenda*, *The Young in Heart*, and *Made For Each Other*.

In 1939, most credits were given at the whim of the producer, and in taking Menzies and Cosgrove out of the usual scrolldown of technical credits—cinematographer, costume designer, art director, film editor—Selznick was acknowledging the importance of both men to *Gone With the Wind*. If Menzies was Selznick's paintbrush, dictating mood through his use of color and composition, Cosgrove was Selznick's architect, building on celluloid a virtual reality that didn't exist. There were more than one hundred trick shots in *Gone With the Wind*. Without the three years of color experience and experiments that preceded the movie, Cosgrove and Slifer could not have successfully created them.

Cosgrove, like Menzies, was a heavy drinker. "Between the two of them we had a hell of a time getting them on the set, but once they were on the set they were pros," said Ridgeway Callow, one of the two assistant directors on *Gone With the Wind*.

Cosgrove did his paintings on glass. He would paint sky, smoke, flames, ruined buildings, cornices, trees, mountains, meadows, columns—anything that was too expensive or too difficult to build or photograph—and then the 30" × 40" glass paintings, the "Cosgrove shots" as they were called, were blended with what the directors had photographed on a sound stage or on location. Cosgrove painted while standing on a tall ladder. "He was one of the greatest artists in the business and he was a drunk and I was always afraid that he was going to fall off," said Hal Kern, the lead film editor on *Gone With the Wind*.

In 1936, while Cosgrove and Slifer were working on *The Garden of Allah*, Selznick sent Cosgrove the galleys of the book he had just bought and told him to read it. While Cosgrove painted, Slifer read *Gone With the Wind*. When Cosgrove climbed down from his ladder so that Slifer could photograph his paintings, Cosgrove read.

Facing page: Jack Cosgrove, the head of Selznick's special effects department, created hundreds of trick shots, which today are known as Special Effects. Without Cosgrove's work, Gone With the Wind *would not have had its epic visual quality. Above: Art director Lyle Wheeler (left) turned Menzies's sketches into master drawings that served as blueprints for the movie's ninety sets. Wilbur G. Kurtz (right), an amateur historian with an encyclopedic knowledge of Georgia's part in the Civil War, brought verisimilitude to the movie's wagons, carriages, and crockery. He also brought the original plans for the 300-foot-long, barrel-vaulted train shed built in 1853. In the movie's famous pull-back shot, thousands of Confederate soldiers lie, wounded and dying, in front of the shed.*

By the next SIP color movie, *A Star Is Born*, Slifer had designed better painting easels, camera pedestals with movable camera mounts, and a new tripod head for glass shots.

Sidney Howard, who had come to Hollywood to work with Selznick and Cukor on the second draft of his screenplay for *Gone With the Wind*, saw a preview of *A Star Is Born* in April 1937, and wrote his wife, Polly, that "it's the first color picture I have seen in which color seemed to me to help rather than to hinder." Four days later he wrote her that "Sam Goldwyn, on the strength of *A Star Is Born*, wants me to make him a color picture. Color, my children, has now been made a fact."

For *The Adventures of Tom Sawyer*, Slifer had an innovative projector for miniatures built; the new projector was combined with an optical printer Slifer had improvised to make glass shots easier and more realistic looking. Because Technicolor film was so slow, it required four times as much light as black-and-white film. Daylight photography was possible, but night and shadowy effects looked murky. Slifer and Cosgrove went to the lamp division of General Electric which developed a 7,000-watt projector bulb for them and sent them 500-watt photo floods, light bulbs so new that they were not yet being manufactured.

"Slowly we were getting the necessary tools to do the effects for GWTW," Slifer wrote.

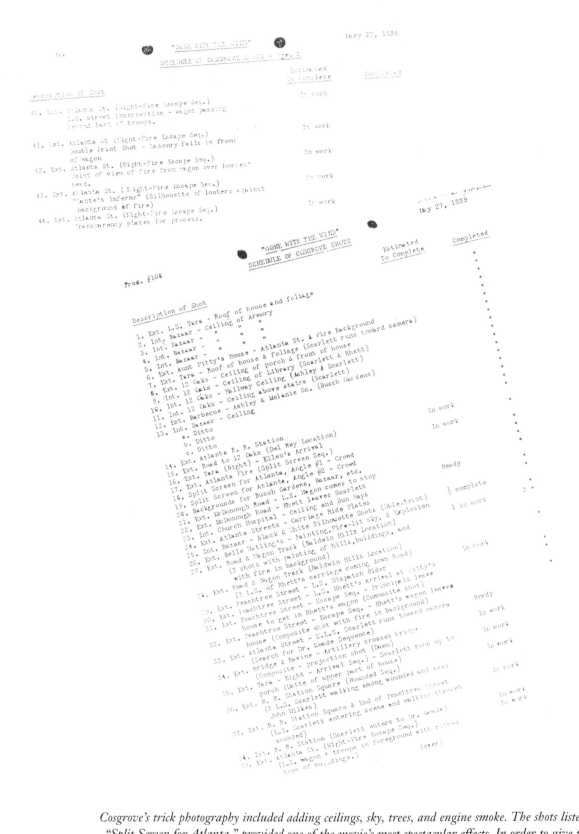

Cosgrove's trick photography included adding ceilings, sky, trees, and engine smoke. The shots listed as 18 and 19, "Split Screen for Atlanta," provided one of the movie's most spectacular effects. In order to give the impression of a huge crowd waiting in front of the newspaper office for news from the battle of Gettysburg, Cosgrove photographed two hundred extras standing on one side of the set. Then he had them change their costumes and move to the other side where he photographed them again. When the two pieces of film were put together, it seemed that every citizen of Atlanta was in the square.

The matte and process photography by Jack Cosgrove and the artists he supervised on *Gone With the Wind* would cost $86,000, $55,000 over budget. On some strips of film, there were as many as four paintings. For example, the shot of Scarlett and her father silhouetted at the top of the hill after Gerald has told his daughter that land is the only thing that matters contains separate matte paintings of Tara, the sky, and the huge tree combined with film of the two live figures.

To take a simpler example, on the first day of principal photography, January 26, 1939, a Cosgrove shot was to be combined with Vivien Leigh running down the driveway in front of Tara. Thirty feet of test film was run off before and after every take, because the sun and shadows were constantly shifting. When Take Three was approved, the film was sent to Technicolor for rewinding. Technicolor, which owned all its cameras and rented them to studios, had absolute control over the processing of its film, and Selznick was constantly fighting Technicolor's desire to do every movie the same way. Selznick always demanded more natural lighting, "which meant that every reel in a Selznick film took Technicolor twice as long to process," said Lyle Wheeler.

That first day, the shot of Tara that would be enhanced by a matte painting of the roof was traced upon a 30" × 40" sheet of Masonite painted Technicolor grey. "The matte line was also indicated," Slifer wrote. "The next step was to draw upon the masonite the portion of Tara that had not been built. Preliminary colors and shade samples were painted upon the masonite."

When the rewound scene of Vivien Leigh running to meet her father was returned to the Cosgrove department the next day, the drawn scene was color matched to the live action. One complication in 1939 was that three-strip Technicolor cameras shot three separate rolls of film—blue, red, and green exposures—called a group. "As each group was placed on or taken off this camera," Slifer said, "it had to be carefully synced to keep the three films in register and also the proper footage noted to keep the films in sync for action." By the time that first matte was completed and ready to be sent to the laboratory a week later, Cukor had been fired. The matte was useless, since the scene was to be rephotographed by Victor Fleming.

Six weeks earlier, when Cukor was still the official director of *Gone With the Wind*, it was Bill Menzies who directed the Burning. On the night of December 10, 1938, Cukor was simply a spectator.

It was Menzies and Wheeler who came up with the idea of burning the old sets—they had to be cleared away so that Tara, Peachtree Street, and the Atlanta railroad station could be built—and making a spectacle of the burning. Typically, Selznick vacillated. "M-G-M has predicted that our photographing of the burning sets will prove to have very little value to us," he wrote on November 20, 1938. M-G-M—which had provided Clark Gable and $1.25 million in return for 50 percent of the profits and the right to distribute *Gone With the Wind*—had urged Selznick to follow the usual path and create the fire in miniature. If the M-G-M executives were right, worried Selznick, going ahead with the burning would be "a reflection on us."

Duly warned, Menzies shrugged off the warning. Bill Menzies wasn't timid. "He was the man who protested against Selznick when Selznick said to meet him at seven o'clock at night in his office and Selznick showed up at nine," said assistant director Ridgeway Callow. The way Callow told the story, as soon as Selznick arrived his butler brought the studio boss his dinner. "None of us had eaten, and he ate in front of us." The next night Menzies announced that instead of waiting for Selznick to arrive, he was going to dinner, and the rest of the technical staff followed him to a Chinese restaurant across the street from the studio. "At eight-thirty the phone rang and a secretary said that Mr. Selznick was waiting for us," said Callow. "So we made him wait another half hour while we finished our dinner."

Selznick probably wasn't aware of his bad manners. "He was really very like King Louis in France," said his secretary, Marcella Rabwin. "Somebody always had to have his brand of cigarettes on him." One of the events to which Selznick was late was Rabwin's wedding, which delayed the ceremony for half an hour. "You had to have a streak of masochism if you worked for him," said Rabwin, who wonders how she survived "some of the unthinking cruelties that he heaped not only on me but on everybody."

Unlike Selznick, most of the other studio chiefs were deliberately cruel, and none were as quickly remorseful and apologetic as David. That was one reason people stayed. There were other reasons, too. "David Selznick was a man with exquisite taste in picture making," said his studio production manager, Raymond Klune. "Even though there were stories that came along that could have and undoubtedly would have made a profit, if they didn't measure up to his taste and standards, he wanted no part of them."

In the case of the burning of Atlanta, Selznick agonized about losing face but, in the end, gave in to his technical people—Menzies, Wheeler, and Ray Klune, who was also production manager on *Gone With the Wind*. The spectacle that they created is always referred to as "the burning of Atlanta," but it was not the actual burning of the city by General Sherman in November 1864. What they filmed was the night two months earlier when the retreating Confederate army torched the ammunition dumps to keep the Union army from capturing them.

The sequence required artistic daring combined with the technical precision of a rocket launch. The big, clumsy Technicolor cameras had to do a ballet of precision moves since it would take less time to move the cameras than to change the camera lenses. A way would have to be figured out to stop the fires while the cameras were moved. And the timing would have to be split second.

A model of the set was built, with every camera move plotted so that the number one camera moved from position six to position nine and a camera with a different lens moved to position six. "Because we wanted to get a medium shot, a long shot, and a close shot from almost every position," said Klune, who handled the logistics. Then, for a week before December 10, the seven three-man camera crews rehearsed. "That was worked out as precisely, as scientifically, as if we'd had computers," Klune said. "We knew that we had probably a maximum of one hour for the burn."

Two sets of pipes were laid to the buildings that would be burned. The fire was fed with coal oil mixed with kerosine, and then electric valves were turned, cutting off the oil and allowing water to rush through the other pipes and smother the flames. "We figured that we wouldn't get more than three burns," Klune said. "We actually got four."

Wilbur Kurtz, who had become friends with Margaret Mitchell in 1935 when she asked him to check the accuracy of her account of the battle of Atlanta, brought an outsider's eye to the week of preparation. On December 6, Kurtz lunched with Selznick, the technical staff, and George Cukor who eyed the large bowl of soup in front of Selznick and said anyone could tell Selznick owned the studio by the size of the bowl. "The impressive fact is that no detail is too small to engage the Selznick interest," Kurtz wrote in his diary. "He wanted to know every move of Rhett, Scarlett and the wagon, down toward Five Points and the railroad. We must have kept it up until nearly 4 o'clock. . . . These conferences work out physical sequences as well as the why or wherefore of them, the psychology of them being paramount."

On December 8, Kurtz drove to the studio back lot, where railroad tracks and freight cars

Three of the seven Technicolor cameras shooting the burning of Atlanta's munitions depots on December 10, 1938, were housed in this corrugated metal shed (The Fred A. Parrish Collection).

made of wood but aged to look like metal were already in place. He ducked beneath the set to see the equipment that would pull down the warehouse wall during the final burn. "The various steel cables join near a central pulley and far out of the sight line, a tractor will furnish the 'yank' that will heave over the wall."

On December 9, Kurtz watched the dress rehearsal. "If Eliza crossing the ice is the big scene in Uncle Tom—these fire sequences are to be the big scenes in GWTW," he wrote.

Everyone who worked at the studio was there on December 10 to watch the burning and to eat baked potatoes, spaghetti, turkey-a-la-king, and red apples at tables inside a North African village built for *The Garden of Allah*. Secretaries and executives sat next to the firemen who were to protect Culver City from David's folly. Or from David's party. Once he had agreed to the burning, Selznick had invited everyone, including his brother, Myron. And Myron was bringing an old client—Laurence Olivier—and a potential new client—Vivien Leigh.

It is fitting that David first saw Leigh framed in the dying flames because, more than anyone else on the movie, Vivien Leigh was burning—with love for Olivier, for whom she had left her husband and five-year-old daughter; with passion for acting; with a willful determination to be Scarlett O'Hara that matched Scarlett's own ruthlessness. From Leigh's carefully applied professional makeup to the mink coat that fell open to show her tiny waist to the way the fire sparked in her green eyes, there was nothing accidental about the time and place of that meeting.

For two years David had searched the country for his Scarlett. If Vivien Leigh had surfaced earlier, she probably would not have gotten the role, because Selznick, the procrastinator, would have had time for second thoughts. He had seen one of her early films and had been unimpressed. But now the need for actors and the beginning of principal photography were only six weeks away.

Did Myron sculpt the meeting because he knew his brother, the romantic, would fall for the drama of the moment? Or did Vivien, who had followed her married lover to Hollywood, conspire with Olivier to put the idea in Myron's head? In either case, fall David did. Years later, he would say discovering Vivien was just like the movie he had made, *A Star Is Born*.

Preparations for the burning had started at 4:00 P.M. with grips, electricians, property men, cameramen, and firemen swarming over the Forty Acres. The burn was set for 8:00 P.M.—after the ninety minute dinner break—and for once Selznick wasn't late. He arrived in a limousine with George Cukor just before eight. But the start was delayed anyway, while David waited for his brother.

Then Menzies gave the signal. Fires were lit on asbestos tables in front of the white and amber floodlights, and the seven cameras began to turn. Black smoke from the tables streamed across the field of light, making the foreground leap in irregular and fast moving patches of shadow. And the two wagons—each with a phony Rhett Butler and a phony Scarlett O'Hara—criss-crossed the blazing set. Both buckboards had stunt drivers hidden inside the wagon box to do the actual driving.

What must Vivien Leigh have thought as she watched the scene she had read so many times in Margaret Mitchell's book and had so often dreamed about playing? We know what Wilbur Kurtz thought. He wrote that, during the burning, he had noticed an attractive girl whom he thought "might be a personage." When the show was over, he asked Marcella Rabwin to tell him the girl's name. Marcella whispered, "Vivien Leigh. Mr. Selznick is seriously considering her." Kurtz watched Selznick walk off the set holding Vivien Leigh by the arm.

The serious consideration had begun when David looked at Vivien in the firelight. Later, he would say that she had looked as he imagined Scarlett would look. By midnight, she was reading for George Cukor in his office.

One of the first scenes Vivien read for Cukor was the scene in the Twelve Oaks library where Scarlett tells Ashley she loves him and is rebuffed. Cukor later said that Vivien had an indescribable wildness about her that no other actress came close to matching.

A hundred actresses had read for the part of Scarlett O'Hara, and three dozen had been given screen tests. By December 10, the choice had narrowed down to Paulette Goddard, Joan Bennett, and Jean Arthur. Cukor and Selznick added the name of Vivien Leigh to that short list. Between December 16 and December 23, all four finalists did screen tests of the scene where Mammy dresses Scarlett for the barbecue, the library scene, and the paddock scene where Scarlett begs Ashley to run away with her.

"They tested her from hell to highwater," said Marcella Rabwin. "They tested her with wardrobe and with makeup and with everything you can think of. There wasn't a shot, there wasn't a test shot of her that wasn't just absolutely perfect. Part of it has to do with the fact that she really had a lot of Scarlett in her." By Christmas Day, Vivien Leigh had the role.

The burning cost $24,715, just $323 over the amount budgeted for it.

When Menzies wrote about the fire afterward, he said he had tried to reduce the colors to great masses of red and black. He had put orange light in the foreground so that the escape from Atlanta would be differentiated from the sequence that followed it when Rhett and Scarlett met the ragged Confederate soldiers on the road out of town and the glare from the distant fire was "accentuated with orange filters with cool high lights on the off side from the fire."

Victor Fleming and members of the wardrobe and makeup crew prepare Vivien Leigh and Clark Gable for Rhett and Scarlett's daring escape. The actors mimed the escape months after the special effects footage was shot.

The look of burning and of the deadness that follows burning is everywhere in *Gone With the Wind*. The movie is, emotionally, all black and red/yellow/orange, beginning with the intensity of the hot late afternoon when Melanie thrashes in childbirth to the fire that rages across Atlanta to the burned-out Twelve Oaks amid acres of blackened grass through the violent yellow and red dawn sky that serves as background to Scarlett's vow that she will survive.

And if that look was provided by Bill Menzies, it was perfected by David Selznick, who demanded retake after retake when the color disappointed him or he felt a trick shot seemed fake. "Fakey," he would say, "phoney." Two days after the Atlanta premiere of the movie, when it was too late to do anything about it, he was agonized because there were still two "phoney looking" shots in the film—one of them the arrival of the carriages at Twelve Oaks for the barbecue. It was a pity, he telegrammed, that "the first two Cosgrove shots in picture are so poor in view of the extraordinary quality of his work through picture as a whole."

Selznick's goal, said Hal Kern, was a movie that would be "absolutely modern" twenty-five years later. "Those were his words to me. He says, 'Hal, I want a picture that if it's reissued twenty-five years from now, will be just as modern as they make pictures then.'"

Selznick was old beyond his sixty-three years in 1965. He would die in June. But he had lived long enough to see how modern his movie looked twenty-five years after the Atlanta premiere. If he were here to see how impressive it looks nearly sixty years later, he would probably have enough hubris not to be surprised.

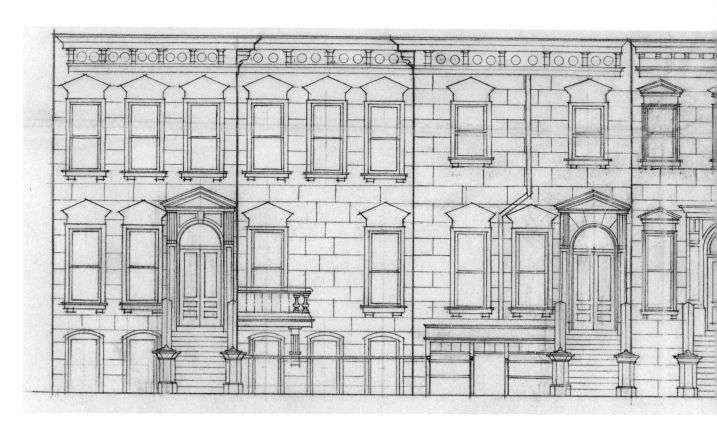

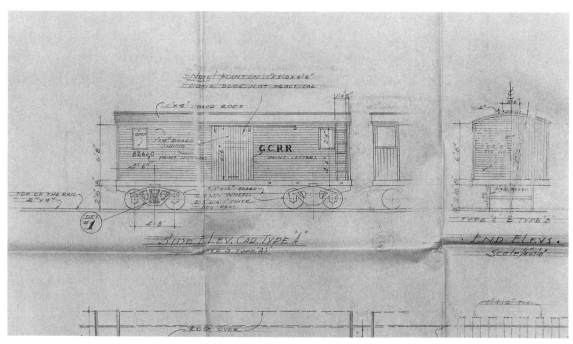

In preparation for the burning, the old sets were hidden by new wooden facades. Many, as is evident from the note on the construction drawing of the stairway, were rough and dangerous. The railroad cars were built of wood that had been painted and aged to look like metal. Wilbur Kurtz made sure that the lettering on the boxcars was historically accurate.

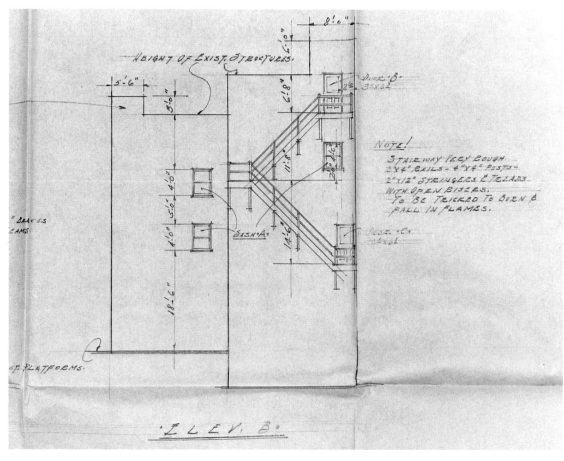

NOTE!
STAIRWAY VERY ROUGH.
2"X4" RAILS - 4"X4" POSTS -
2"X12" STRINGERS & TREADS
WITH OPEN RISERS.
TO BE TRICKED TO BURN &
FALL IN FLAMES.

HEIGHT OF EXIST. STRUCTURES.

'ELEV. B.'

This photograph by Fred Parrish follows one labeled, "D.O.S. before the fire starts"; it is identified as "The fire is slated" (The Fred A. Parrish Collection). Within a minute, kerosene would pour through the pipes, and the fire, which was planned out by explosives expert Lee Zavits, would erupt again. "It was a brave affair," Kurtz wrote in his journal. "The leaping flames appeared above the line of boxcars and licked hungrily at the old King Kong set."

Of the two hundred continuity sketches by Menzies and his staff that remain in the Selznick Archive, sixty-six depict the fire sequence. These unsigned and undated watercolor storyboards give the feel of the sequence as it appeared in the film but differ in most details, since the script was changed after the drawings were made. The storyboard above, showing the escape from the city by Rhett and Scarlett, has extra long drawings because Selznick originally intended to show the fire sequence on a screen that was double the normal width. Clarence Slifer devised a two-camera and mirror setup that was used on the night of the fire to get a wide-screen effect, but the idea was later dropped. Both Jock Whitney and M-G-M considered it an unnecessary gimmick. Selznick did not give up on the idea of wide-screen, however. Nine years later, he created the first wide-screen effects for the storm-at-sea climax of Portrait of Jennie for the movie's initial engagements.

"PEACHTREE STREET
Toward CAMERA comes the horse at a lope, the wagon swaying behind it as it bumps over the ruts.
The horse and the wagon and the people in it are only dim figures in the semi-darkness under the trees."
Gone With the Wind *screenplay*

Of the two hundred continuity sketches by Menzies and his staff that remain in the Selznick Archive, sixty-six depict the fire sequence. These unsigned and undated watercolor storyboards give the feel of the sequence as it appeared in the film but differ in most details, since the script was changed after the drawings were made. The storyboard above, showing the escape from the city by Rhett and Scarlett, has extra long drawings because Selznick originally intended to show the fire sequence on a screen that was double the normal width. Clarence Slifer devised a two-camera and mirror setup that was used on the night of the fire to get a wide-screen effect, but the idea was later dropped. Both Jock Whitney and M-G-M considered it an unnecessary gimmick. Selznick did not give up on the idea of wide-screen, however. Nine years later, he created the first wide-screen effects for the storm-at-sea climax of Portrait of Jennie for the movie's initial engagements.

114

As early as December 1937, Selznick was exploring the idea of using a wide screen during the fire sequence. As he wrote to his New York story editor, Kay Brown, on December 20, it would give the audience "the sense that they were actually in the middle of the fire and in the middle of the evacuation." Selznick had become intrigued with a two-camera system that Fred Waller was planning to create for the 1939 New York World's Fair. Waller later modified his system into the three-camera Cinerama which was introduced in 1952, four years after Selznick used wide-screen in Portrait of Jennie.

*"247 BURNING BUILDING AND BOXCAR —
FROM THEIR ANGLE*
Only a few feet beyond the boxcar is a flaming building. Sparks,
embers, and bits of burning wood are showering the boxcar.
Carry over this SOUND of Prissy's scream."
        Gone With the Wind *screenplay*
        (Scene rendering: Collection Dennis A. Shaw and James Tumblin)

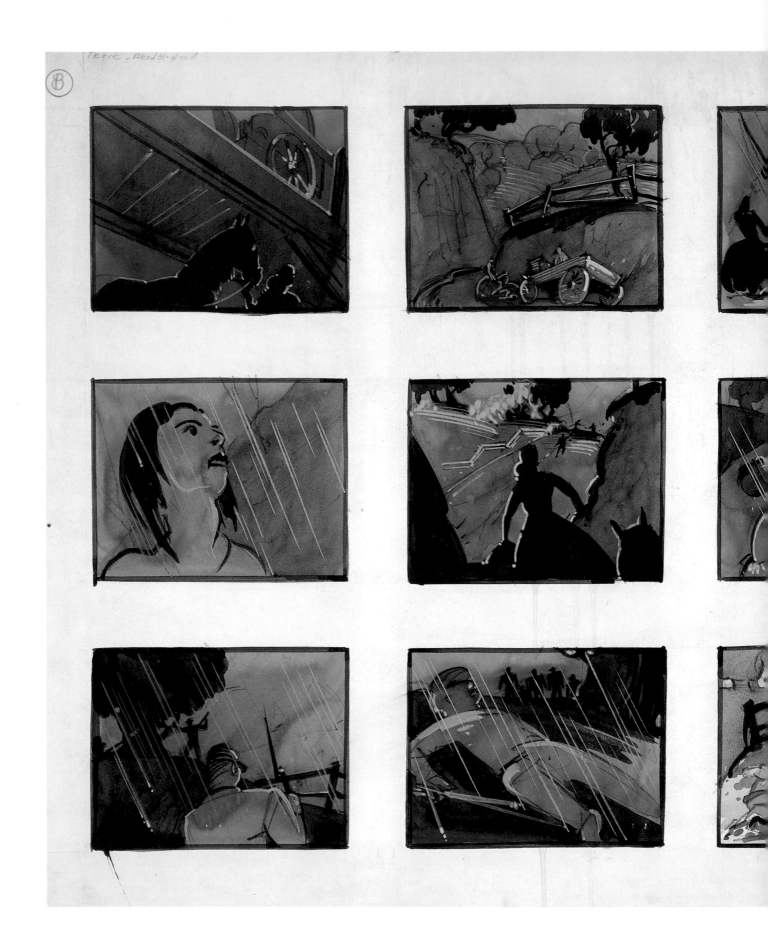

Tree - Bridge - Road

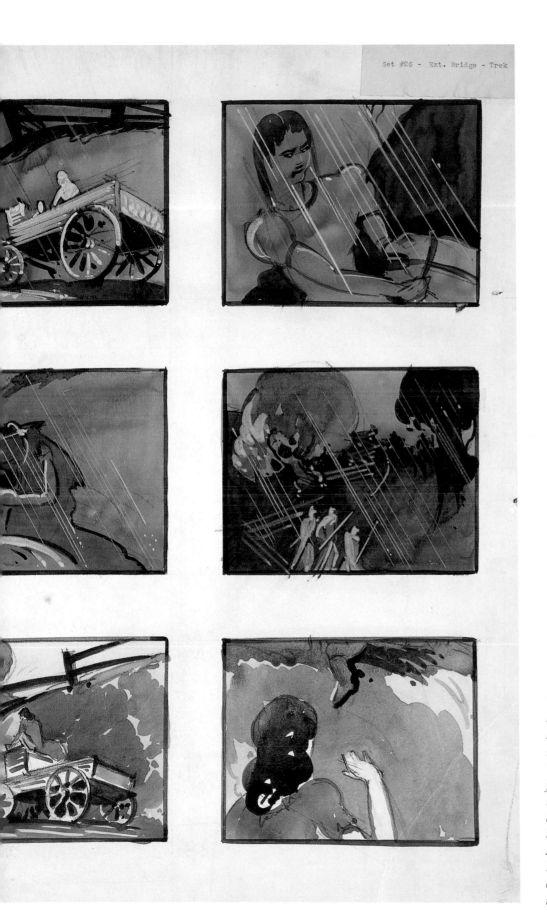

This twelve-panel storyboard details Scarlett's trek home to Tara after Rhett has left to join the retreating Confederate soldiers. The panel in which Scarlett hides from the Union troops by pulling the horse and wagon under the bridge, coincides with the movie's Shot 272 "EXT. AT BRIDGE AND SWAMP (GREENISH RAIN EFFECT)." None of the other panels corresponds to shots in the film.

This scene rendering of the reflection of the Union soldiers in the water under the bridge was drawn by Jack Martin Smith, as was the sketch of Prissy and Scarlett hiding under the bridge on page 126. It is likely that Smith also drew the two unsigned drawings on page 127. Smith, a 1934 graduate of the University of Southern California School of Architecture, was borrowed from M-G-M, where his previous assignment had been sketch artist on The Wizard of Oz. Later, at 20th Century-Fox, Smith would share Academy Awards for art direction on Cleopatra, Fantastic Voyage, and Hello, Dolly.

"*The rain falling on her terrified face. We hear the rumble of horses' hooves and artillery wheels passing over the wooden bridge above her. CAMERA (ON BOOM) PULLS BACK until we see that the wagon with Prissy, Melanie, and the baby is in a swamp under a bridge. Scarlett stands at the horse's bridle, knee-deep in the green slime of the swamp. . . . In continuous movement, CAMERA NOW TILTS UPWARD until it includes the lower portion of artillery wheels passing overhead on the wooden bridge.*"

Gone With the Wind *screenplay*

127

Many of the sketches of Scarlett's trip home are painted in deep blue colors. "On the approach to Tara the backings were indigo with pure silhouette effects in front to get vibration and the effect of low visibility," Menzies wrote in his notes. Like the reflections of the Union soldiers on pages 124–125, Scarlett pulling the horse past Union pickets (right) was not in the film. Scenes such as these may have been shot but then winnowed out in the editing room when the movie was cut by almost an hour after the first preview.

129

The unsigned scene rendering at upper left on the facing page, with its pastoral colors, is in unexplained contrast to a dozen dark and somber drawings of the devastated Wilkes plantation, the most arresting of which is the dead man draped over the fence at Twelve Oaks (above), drawn by Frank Powers.

Above: This sketch of the interior of the burned house is signed Dorothea Holt. Facing page: The scene rendering of Scarlett (visible near the arch at the right) entering the ruined Twelve Oaks was drawn by "Mac" Johnson. These two drawings offer an unusual comparison of how the movie's two chief sketch artists handled almost identical material. Johnson tended to stylize his drawings, while Holt's sketches were more realistic. The ruined Twelve Oaks was not a set but a hanging miniature. While Vivien Leigh stood on a concrete floor, special effects men standing on a ladder shot down at her through a five-foot model of the house.

"EXT.   GROUNDS OF TARA . . .
*Deep ruts and furrows were cut into the road where
horses had dragged heavy guns along it and the red
gullies on either side were deeply gashed by the wheels.
The cotton was mangled and trampled where cavalry
and infantry, forced off the narrow road, had marched
through the green bushes, grinding them into the
earth. Here and there in road and fields lay buckles
and bits of harness leather, canteens flattened by hooves
and caisson wheels, buttons, blue caps, worn socks, bits
of bloody rags, all the litter left by a marching army.*"
Gone With the Wind *screenplay*

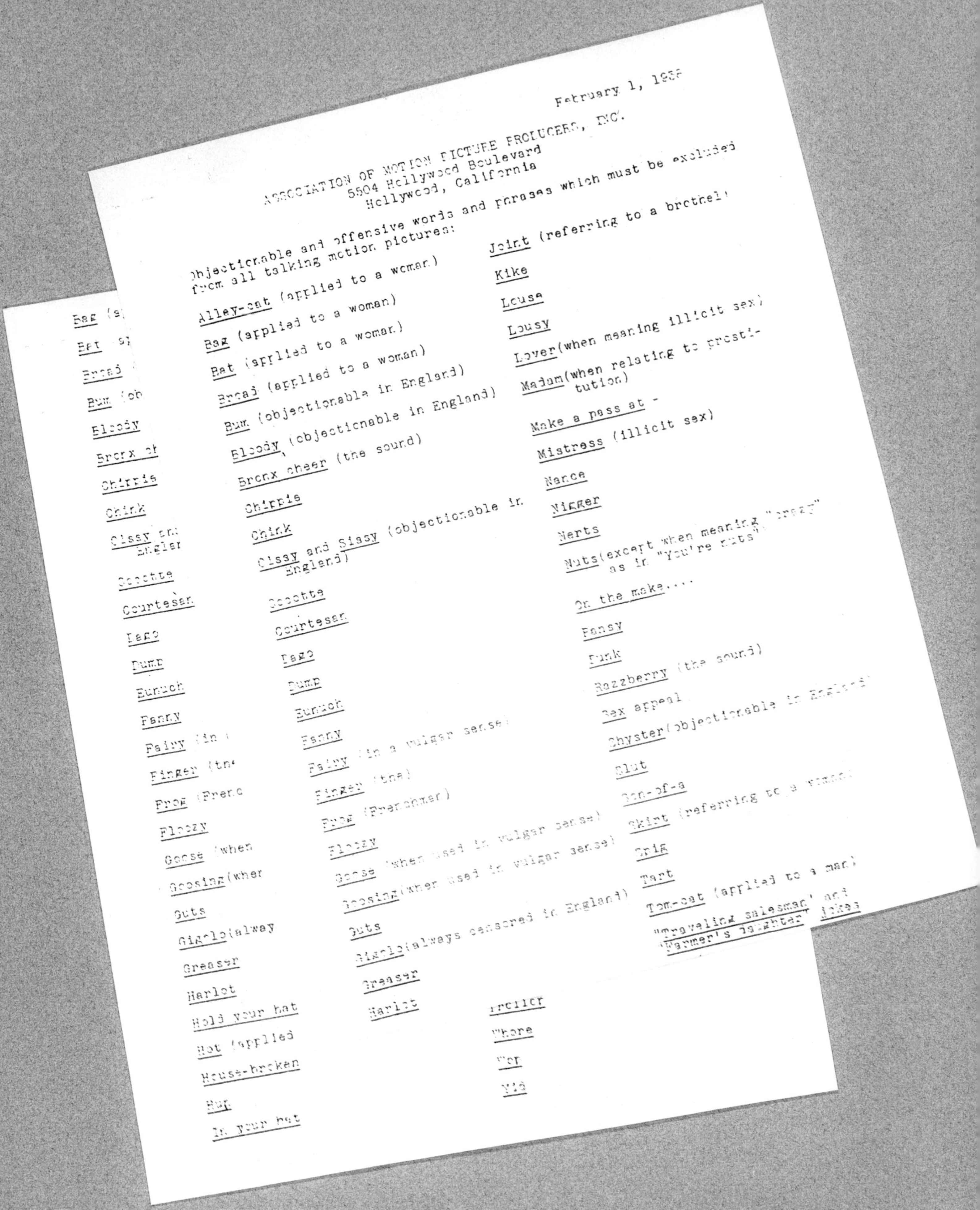

February 1, 1938

ASSOCIATION OF MOTION PICTURE PRODUCERS, INC.
5504 Hollywood Boulevard
Hollywood, California

Objectionable and offensive words and phrases which must be excluded from all talking motion pictures:

Alley-cat (applied to a woman)

Bag (applied to a woman)

Bat (applied to a woman)

Broad (applied to a woman)

Bum (objectionable in England)

Bloody (objectionable in England)

Bronx cheer (the sound)

Chippie

Chink

Cissy and Sissy (objectionable in England)

Cocotte

Courtesan

Lag

Dump

Eunuch

Fanny

Fairy (in a vulgar sense)

Finger (the)

Frog (Frenchman)

Floozy

Goose (when used in vulgar sense)

Goosing (when used in vulgar sense)

Guts

Gigolo (always censored in England)

Greaser

Harlot

Joint (referring to a brothel)

Kike

Louse

Lousy

Lover (when meaning illicit sex)

Madam (when relating to prostitution)

Make a pass at -

Mistress (illicit sex)

Nance

Nigger

Nerts

Nuts (except when meaning "crazy" as in "You're nuts")

On the make....

Pansy

Punk

Razzberry (the sound)

Sex appeal

Shyster (objectionable in England)

Slut

Son-of-a

Skirt (referring to a woman)

Trib

Tart

Tom-cat (applied to a man) and "traveling salesman" and "farmer's daughter" jokes

Trollop

Whore

Wop

Yid

Bag (s
Bat (s
Broad
Bum (ob
Bloody
Bronx ch
Chippie
Chink
Cissy and Sissy
Cocotte
Courtesan
Lag
Dump
Eunuch
Fanny
Fairy (in
Finger (the
Frog (Frenc
Floozy
Goose (when
Goosing (when
Guts
Gigolo (alway
Greaser
Harlot
Hold your hat
Hot (applied
House-broken
Hus
In your hat

CENSORSHIP:
Everyone Except Rhett Butler Gave a Damn

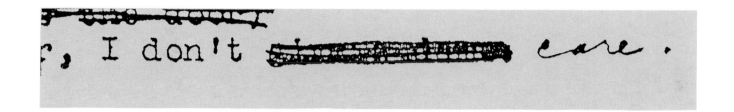

The censors first paid attention to *Gone With the Wind* in September 1937—sixteen months before the movie started shooting. As usual, the anxieties of the Production Code Administration centered on sex—implicit, explicit, or illicit—and the consequences of sex. After reading one of the early scripts, Joseph Breen, the Code administrator, sent David Selznick a seven-page letter expressing his concern because the script had too much discussion of childbirth and pregnancy. The pregnancy of Melanie Wilkes bothered Breen despite the fact that Melanie was a genteel and properly married Southern lady. Melanie's childbirth, Breen warned, must not be "gruesome."

Americans in 1937 may not have believed that babies were brought by storks, but the movie industry's Production Code guarded them against alternative explanations. The Code—which was Hollywood's self-censorship in response to threats of a boycott from the Catholic church—had been enforced since 1934 when Catholic bishops formed the Legion of Decency. The studios had two choices: censor themselves or have Catholic priests bar their parishioners from going to all movies.

The Code expressed a small town morality, and America was still a nation of small cities and small towns where almost everyone went to church on Sunday. "Ministers of religion," said the Code, should not be used as villains. Profanity—including the words "Lord," "God," "Jesus," "Christ," "Gawd," "hell," and "damn"—was forbidden. The first sentence of the Code said it all: "No picture shall be produced which will lower the moral standards of those who see it." And the moral standards to be enforced were those of Catholics and conservative Protestants.

The Production Code Administration was also called the Hays Office after Will Hays, an elder in the Presbyterian church and a former Postmaster General to President Warren

Facing page: More than words were forbidden. Under the Production Code, no movie was allowed to show white slavery, miscegenation, lustful embraces, childbirth, sub-machine guns, or law enforcement officers dying at the hands of criminals. Above: Detail from page 249 of the script for Gone With the Wind.

Harding. Hays, who had powerful Republican connections, had been hired by the industry to head the Motion Picture Producers and Distributors Association of America in 1921 when the debauchery pictured in movies and lived by movie stars had put Hollywood under threat of federal censorship. Four decades later, in 1966, the industry would similarly hire Jack Valenti, a special assistant to President Lyndon Johnson, to head the motion picture association and create a "voluntary" ratings system for the use of parents.

Neither the men who made the movies nor the men who enforced the Code were unsophisticated. So the battles between Joseph Ignatius Breen and the president of Selznick International Pictures were also games in which each man said one thing but often thought another. In response to Breen's letter, Selznick assured his story editor, Val Lewton, "that we will not have as much trouble with Breen as his letter would indicate." Selznick said he had spoken to Breen, and "Joe made clear himself that he would fight on our side in this case."

A little flattery from a studio head never hurt. After Lewton submitted a different draft of Sidney Howard's script to the Code office in February 1938, he urged Selznick to use his considerable charm on Breen. "It is my strong conviction that if you will give Mr. Breen an hour of your time after he has read *Gone With the Wind*, we will be able to secure twice as many concessions from him as if I, myself, were to carry on this negotiation," Lewton wrote his boss. "Believe me, I am not passing the buck. For the ordinary picture and the ordinary problem I feel I am adequate, but in this case where I know, for instance, that Breen would throw out the word 'belch' and you might want to keep it in, I do think it best for you to see him."

Some of the censors saw themselves carrying lance and shield as defenders of purity in an impure world. Joe Breen wasn't one of them. He had been a newspaper reporter in Chicago and a public relations man for the Catholic Church. He had china blue eyes that might have inspired the writer of *When Irish Eyes Are Smiling*, a large number of children, a Malibu beach house, and a penchant for the liberal use of the word, "fuck." Jack Vizzard, a sub-censor who had come to Hollywood straight from a Jesuit seminary, once asked Breen about his crude language. Breen said he had been polite when he first came to Hollywood, "and they thought I was a sissy. I had to show them I meant what I said."

When Lewton sent Breen the shooting script of *Gone With the Wind* a few days before the movie started production, Breen responded: "I regret to be compelled to advise you that this material, in our judgement, is unacceptable under the provisions of the production code and cannot be approved."

Breen began his six-page critique of the script with a lecture: "Please note the statement in the Code, referring to married love, that 'the passion arising from this love is not the proper subject for plots,' and that the presentation on the screen of the sexual relationship of the married life 'must not excite sexual reactions, mental or physical.'" Then he got down to specifics. Scarlett could not press her body against Ashley, "a married man." The apparent rape of Scarlett by her husband Rhett Butler must be eliminated. Since words were as sinful as deeds, also to be eliminated were Rhett's speech, "I still want you more than any woman I've ever seen," and Melanie's line, 'I know I shall die when my baby comes. The doctors warned me not to have another.'"

Breen was particularly concerned with Belle Watling, Margaret Mitchell's good-hearted prostitute. Prostitution may have flourished in America, but it wasn't allowed to exist in that not quite mirror image of the real world—the movies. A woman selling her virtue was item six in Section XII: Repellent Subjects. And a February 1938 list of "Objectionable and offensive words and phrases which must be excluded from all talking motion pictures" included the words "chippie," "cocotte," "courtesan," "floozy," "mistress," "slut," "tart," "whore," and "Madam (relating to prostitution)."

Such "establishments" as the one over which Belle presided "suggest to the average person, at once, sex, or sin, or they excite unwholesome or morbid curiosity in the minds of youth," Breen warned. Worse—much worse—"the character of Belle—a prostitute—is made to appear highly sympathetic, and to be 'admired' in contrast to the decent women of your story."

For the next five months, as new scenes were written and old ones rewritten and then rewritten again, Selznick and the censors continued to skirmish over Belle Watling. There was an unacceptable suggestion of illicit intimacy between Rhett and Belle. There was an unacceptable inference that Belle ran a brothel. "We suggest that Belle is the proprietress of the saloon," Breen wrote on March 31.

Breen was less formal in his private discussions with the makers of *Gone With the Wind*. As Val Lewton wrote to Selznick on April 7: "Mr. Breen goes to the bathroom every morning. He does not deny that he does so or that there is such a place as the bathroom, but he feels that neither his actions nor the bathroom are fit subjects for screen entertainment. This is the essence of the Hays' office attitude toward prostitution, at least as Joe told it to me in somewhat cruder language."

The lines to which Breen objected were eliminated. Belle no longer combed Rhett's hair, and he no longer wore a dressing gown in her presence. Her "establishment" was identified only as a saloon.

Neither audiences nor the Legion of Decency were fooled. Ona Munson's ripe presence on the screen as Belle needed no words. The Catholic Church rated *Gone With the Wind* "objectionable in part," and specifically criticized "the attractive portrayal of the immoral character of a supporting role in the story."

It would be wrong to see the Production Code Administration and the movie executives as enemies. Movies had begun as rowdy entertainment for poor immigrants in big cities; and the makers of movies would spend the next ninety years trying to appear respectable. From 1905, when nickelodeons were accused of leading to the moral decline of the working class, to 1995, when Senator Robert Dole made headlines by denouncing movies as anti-family, the film industry—created and run by immigrants, a large number of whom were Jews—was an easy target. Until 1952, when a Supreme Court decision guaranteed films the right of free speech,[3] there were, at various times, more than a dozen local and state censor boards. Breen's salary was paid by the movie studios. It was his job to keep them from getting into trouble with the Legion of Decency and with Ohio, Virginia, and the other six states and cities that had censor boards in 1939.

In February 1939, as director George Cukor prepared to shoot the birth of Melanie's baby, Lewton wrote the following note to Selznick about the objections of Islin Auster, a code subcensor, to the childbirth sequence. "The only Code violations are the places which show the suffering of childbirth, which they deem as improper entertainment. This includes the showing of all scenes in which Melanie winces with pain, grips the towel, oozes perspiration." Lewton added, "I don't know how seriously you should take all this. If you'd phone him and discuss these matters with him, I am certain he would modify all his objections. On the other hand, I don't know whether this is a safe course to follow or not, inasmuch as state censor boards are very likely to cut some of the material which he advises us not to use."

3. The Supreme Court unanimously gave movies the protection of free speech in the case of Burstyn v. Wilson which concerned Roberto Rossellini's *The Miracle*, an Italian movie that had been banned by New York censors as sacrilegious.

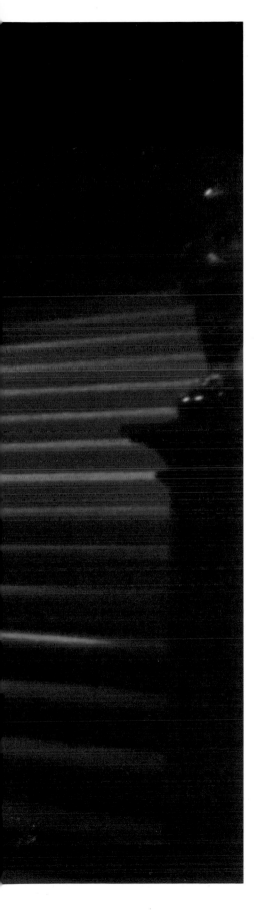

Left: An angry and drunken Rhett carries Scarlett up to bed. Above: When Gone With the Wind *was submitted for a Code seal, Joseph Breen objected to the morning-after scene as "too vivid a portrayal of Scarlett's reactions to the rape." In a memo to Selznick, story editor Val Lewton wrote, "Personally, I feel that the best thing to do is to let him see the film again with his merry men and then for you to enter into the discussion that is bound to follow their viewing of the film." After Breen saw the film a second time, the Code administrator still felt that Scarlett was "lying in bed figuratively licking her chops." Lewton recommended that the problem be tabled until after the second preview, "because we cannot use our little device to get in the 'damn' until after the next preview anyhow." (Two scenes from* Gone With the Wind *© 1939 Turner Entertainment Co. All Rights Reserved. Photo: Photofest)*

Left: "Mac" Johnson has placed a painting of a nude woman on the wall of Belle Watling's parlor, something the Hays office would never have allowed. Above: This scene showing Atlanta's leading madam, played by Ona Munson, giving water to the Confederate wounded was cut from the movie (The Fred A. Parrish Collection). Selznick may have deferred to Production Code Administrator Joseph Breen, who was concerned that an indecent woman had been made too sympathetic.

In the end, Melanie's childbirth had little agony, and the birth of Bonnie Blue Butler to Scarlett wasn't shown at all.

If the long noses of the Code enforcers were alert to the slightest whiff of sex, Breen's more serious job involved the amorphous area known as "political." The Code said that the movies must respect the flag, the American justice system, and natural and human law. They also had to respect the "national feelings" of the countries that comprised Hollywood's foreign market. "Hitler and his government are unfairly represented in this story, in violation of the Code," a censor wrote to Warner Bros. about the script of *Confessions of a Nazi Spy* in 1938. "To represent Hitler only as a screaming madman and a bloodthirsty persecutor and nothing else is manifestly unfair, considering his phenomenal public career, his unchallenged political and social achievement and his position as head of the most important continental European power."

The most delicate "political" problem in *Gone With the Wind* concerned the treatment of its black characters. The polite word in 1939 was "Negroes," but the book and the early scripts were full of references to "niggers." On January 24, two days before the movie started shooting, Breen warned Selznick—not for the first time—that "this word is highly offensive to negroes throughout the United States and will be quite forcefully resented by them."

In a memorandum written for his files on February 9, Breen expressed relief that Selznick had agreed not to use the word. Selznick had been shaken by hundreds of letters from individual Negroes and Negro organizations and by attacks in Negro newspapers. For a year, Margaret Mitchell's 1,037 page novel had been Selznick's bible. He had sent memo after memo telling his screenwriters, his set designers, and his directors to look for answers in what he always called "the book." And now he was discovering that "the book"—with the stalwart Ku Klux Klan defending white womanhood and former slaves who were unhappy at being freed and still devoted to their masters—infuriated Negroes.

"My dear, they want to let the darkies vote!" Melanie's Aunt Pitty prattles in chapter 33, for example. "Did you ever hear of anything more silly? Though—I don't know—now that I think about it, Uncle Peter has much more sense than any Republican I ever saw and much better manners but, of course Uncle Peter is far too well bred to want to vote. But the very notion has upset the darkies till they're right addled."

Margaret Mitchell always said that part of her concern about showing her manuscript to publishers was her awareness that the novel had a Southern point of view. The moral correctness of slavery, for example, was never questioned.

What worried Selznick most during those early weeks of production was that there might be "repercussions not simply on the picture, and not simply upon the company and upon me personally, but on the Jews of America as a whole. . . ." In one of those rambling memos in which he discovered what he was thinking by spilling half-finished thoughts onto paper, Selznick talked of spending $1,500 to hire a Negro college president as a public relations man for the movie. Russell Birdwell, the press agent who had made a national event out of Selznick's two-year search for an actress to play Scarlett O'Hara, had the more sensible idea of treating the black actors in the movie as the picture's stars and sending special portraits of them and articles supposedly written by them to the leading Negro newspapers.

A form letter was also drafted. Selznick International Pictures assured worried blacks that the studio had been "in frequent communication with Mr. Walter White, of the Society for the Advancement of Colored People, and have accepted his suggestions concerning the elimination of the word 'nigger' from our picture. We have, moreover, gone further than this and have portrayed important Negro characters as lovable, faithful, high-typed people—so picturized that they can leave no impression but a very nice one."

But David could never leave well enough alone. "Increasingly I regret the loss of the better negroes being able to refer to themselves as niggers, and other uses of the word nigger by one negro talking about another," he wrote Lewton on June 7, three weeks before the movie ended production. "All the uses that I would have liked to have retained do nothing but glorify the negroes, and I can't believe that we were sound in having a blanket rule of this kind, nor can I believe that we would have offended any negroes if we had used the word 'nigger' with care. . . . It may still not be too late to salvage two or three of these uses."

Along with Joe Breen, Lewton, who would go on to produce such haunting and psychologically disturbing horror films as *Cat People* and *I Walked With a Zombie*, talked Selznick out of resurrecting "nigger." But no one could talk or threaten Selznick out of using another forbidden word.

Margaret Mitchell had ended her novel with Rhett Butler walking out on Scarlett. "If you go, what shall I do?" Scarlett had asked. And Rhett had replied, "My dear, I don't give a damn."

On June 8, 1939, Breen sent the following message to Selznick:

"Scene 681, page 249: Please eliminate the underlined word in the following line: 'Frankly, my dear, I don't give a damn.'"

The next day Lewton sent Selznick a list of alternative lines that included, "I don't give a hoot," "It has become of no concern to me," "It makes my gorge rise," and "My indifference is boundless."

Whenever Breen approved a script, new dialogue, or a new scene, he ended his letter with a warning: "Our final judgments will be based on the finished picture." In the finished picture that was shown to Breen in late September, Rhett Butler said, "Frankly, my dear, I don't care." The power of the Code lay in the granting or withholding of a seal of approval which allowed a movie to be played in theaters. *Gone With the Wind* was given Certificate No. 5729 on September 28, 1939.

That was all Selznick was waiting for. Three weeks earlier he had written Jock Whitney, "I think we ought to fight him [Breen] in connection with the 'Frankly I don't give a damn' line, even to the point of taking it to the Board of Directors. And I think further that if he goes back on any of his consents in connection with other parts of the picture, where, despite his comparatively liberal attitude, we had to make any number of changes, we should fight him until the cows come home, since we have got the perfect story and picture with which to fight him and I think we could make the whole Hays Association ridiculous. However, there is probably no point in creating any issues with him, at least until he has passed *Gone With the Wind* in its present form."

What is fascinating is that Selznick thought seriously of using *Gone With the Wind* to break the Code fourteen years before Otto Preminger dared to release *The Moon Is Blue* without a Code seal. A comedy about adultery with no adultery but some mildly naughty language, *The Moon Is Blue* was distributed by United Artists and was a box office success in 1953. Selznick, too, released most of his pictures through United Artists rather than through one of the major studios which backed the Code, but he was checkmated, in the case of *Gone With the Wind*, by the fact that his contract with M-G-M required a Code seal.

Selznick waited until after his second sneak preview of the movie and then tracked Breen down at a resort where he had gone on vacation. Breen said his hands were chained and padlocked by the Code. It was there in black-and-white. "Damn" was forbidden.

Frequently, however, an industry executive's public posture was not the same as his private deeds. As Lewton wrote to Selznick on October 20, "[Breen]—without prompting from me—told me that our taking the matter up with Hays might establish a precedent which might be

SELZNICK INTERNATIONAL PICTURES, INC.

CULVER CITY, CALIFORNIA

Inter-Office Communication

DATE June 9, 1939

SUBJECT GONE WITH THE WIND

TO Connie Earle, Lydia Schiller, Tillie Thompson

FROM Barbara Keon

This supersedes my note of June 6 on the alternate speech for Scene 681.

Please instead make two alternate ends to this scene besides the corrected version Mr. Selznick and Mr. Fleming devised on the set yesterday. The speeches for these alternate versions will read as follows:

1. Rhett: (very slowly) "Frankly my dear i just -- don't -- care."

2. "I wish I could care what you do or where you go -
(he opens the door)
"But frankly my dear I just don't care."

These are for censorship protection.

BK

BK:ps

CONTINUED (2)   249

          Rhett (with a far-away look; it is a new Rhett
           -now to us and new to him)
I want peace, Scarlett, peace - and a little dignity. I want
to see if there isn't something left in life of charm and
grace...
         (with just a trace of amusement)
Do you know what I'm talking about?

          Scarlett
No. I know that I love you.

          Rhett (picking up his bag)
That's your misfortune.
        (goes toward the door)

          Scarlett (after him)
But, darling, if you go, what shall I do? Where shall I
go?
          Rhett (at the door)
I wish I could care what you do or where you go, but I can't
(opens the door)
Frankly, my dear, I don't care.

    He goes out into the mist, Scarlett looking after him.

    CLOSE SHOT - SCARLETT

    She is left stunned. She looks around, crushed by this
blow, and speaks aloud:

          Scarlett
I can't let him go! There must be some way I can hold him!
(she walks around the room thinking, moving jerkily
and without design)
But I can't think about that now! I'll go crazy if I do!...I'll
think about it tomorrow...

    But the thought of it will not down. She throws herself
on the stairs, defeated, and with nothing to look forward
to. She lies face down with her head on her hands. CAMERA
MOVES UP TO A CLOSE UP of Scarlett sobbing and HOLDS FOR
A MOMENT:

          Scarlett
But I must think about it! I must think about it! What is
there to do? What is there that matters?

    Suddenly on the sound track we hear Gerald's voice:

          Gerald's voice
Do you mean to tell me, Katie Scarlett O'Hara, that Tara
doesn't mean anything to you?

    Scarlett's sobbing ceases. She lifts her tear-stained
face slowly, but does not rise.

          Gerald's voice (continues)
Why, land's the only thing that matters - because it's the
only thing that lasts.

hs   CONTINUED:

GONE WITH THE WIND   LEWTON

"---Frankly, my dear, nothing could interest me less ----" Bowie

  , I don't care -----" Anon.

  , it leaves me cold -----" Ibid.

  , it has become of no concern to me ----" Ibid.

  , I don't give a Continental ----" Ibid.

  , I don't give a hoot!" Ibid.

  , I don't give a whoop!" Ibid.

  , I am completely indifferent ---" Ibid.

  , you can go to the devil, for all of me ---" Ibid.

  , you can go to the devil for all I care ---" Ibid.

  , I'm not even indifferent -- I just don't care --"

  , I've come to the end---" Killington

  , I just don't care ---" L.

  , my indifference is boundless ---" Ibid.

  , I don't give a straw

  , It's all the same to me

  , it is of no consequence

  , the devil may care--- I don't!

  , I've withdrawn from the battle

  , the whole thing is a stench in my nostrils

  , it makes my gorge rise

During the half-century since Gone With the Wind *was released, dialogue that was once considered shocking has become relatively commonplace.*

helpful to him as, personally but not professionally, he agrees that the use of the word 'damn' under certain circumstances such as this one should be permissible. However, he cannot openly support us. . . ."

Lewton drafted a letter from Selznick to Will Hays in which Selznick argued that "even such moral publications as Woman's Home Companion, Saturday Evening Post, Collier's and The Atlantic Monthly, use this word freely." The letter also reminded Hays that Selznick had made such literary movies as *A Tale of Two Cities*, *David Copperfield*, and *Little Lord Fauntleroy*. Besides, the Hays Office had made an exception and allowed the word "damn" to be used in the Warner Bros. short *The Man Without a Country*.

Unfortunately for Selznick, Hays—who had his headquarters in New York—was surrounded by fervent defenders of the status quo. Francis Harmon, the Baptist vice president of the motion picture association, telegraphed Breen demanding that Breen "SEND NIGHT LETTER SETTING FORTH STRONGEST REASONS WHY THE CASES DIFFER." Which Breen—whatever his private feelings—did.

Selznick then appealed to the Board of Directors of the Motion Picture Producers and Distributors Association, many of whom were heads of rival studios. Lewton rounded up telegrams of support from Hal Roach and Sol Lesser, who couldn't go to New York for the meeting on October 27. "Were I present at the meeting I would vote to permit the inclusion of the line in the picture," Lesser wrote after a special screening of the film had been arranged for him.

The Board meeting was, according to an account given to Selznick as soon as the meeting ended, "a very stormy session." At first, Hays was "bitterly opposed" to the word and, beyond the word, to any changes in the Code. Universal, Paramount, and Fox stood with Hays. Nicholas Schenck, the most powerful man at the most powerful studio, M-G-M, stepped forward on Selznick's side. It was up to Schenck to protect his investment.

By the end of the two-hour meeting, Hays had weakened. It was agreed that consideration would be given to amending the Code. Selznick was not authorized to use the word, "damn." But his Code seal was not taken away. In essence, the Hays office looked the other way. Since "damn" was still forbidden, however, Selznick was fined $5,000 for disobeying the Code.

In December 1939, when America watched Rhett Butler turn his back on Scarlett with "Frankly, my dear, I don't give a damn," the country did not topple. If anyone suffered, it was Joe Breen, who was ridiculed in Jimmie Fidler's newspaper column on Christmas day.

"When Hays Office purists saw that naughty, naughty word in the script, they were aghast," Fidler wrote. "What would women's clubs think? What would censors think? What would parents do when they saw the morals of their children toppling over the 'damn?'" Fidler described Breen as "probably the only Irishman in history to be appalled by so mild an expletive." And he added, "The motion picture industry has long outgrown infancy. It's too old now to have its mouth washed with soap."

As for those state and local censors that Breen was defending the industry against, all of them—Pennsylvania, Ohio and New York, Virginia, Detroit, Portland, Kansas, and Chicago—passed the movie without a single qualm or a single cut.

PRODUCTION

I n an era when movies were made fast and cheap, David Selznick waited more than two and a half years to let his actors loose on a sound stage. Yet he still started production with an unfinished script, a barely acquired cast, and half-built sets.

In contrast, after Warner Bros. lost *Gone With the Wind* to Selznick, Jack Warner bought *Jezebel*, a bad play about a willful Southern Belle, and, at a cost of a little over a million dollars, had the movie playing in theaters by March 1938. *Jezebel* starred Bette Davis, who—like nearly every other actress in Hollywood—wanted to play Scarlett O'Hara, and it won Davis her second Academy Award. Selznick was terrified that the magnolia blossoms and southern accents of *Jezebel* would satiate moviegoers, but the film did not even begin to blunt the public's growing appetite for *Gone With the Wind*.

The two-year search for Scarlett had fed that appetite. But, if Selznick's quest was the greatest of publicity stunts, it was also real. Unlike other producers who launched nationwide searches and ended up with stars who just happened to be under contract to them all along, Selznick had actually discovered Freddie Bartholomew for *David Copperfield* and had postponed *The Adventures of Tom Sawyer* until he came across Tommy Kelly, a school janitor's son with no movie experience. Every instinct told Selznick that *Gone With the Wind* would be diminished if he were forced to put a well-known actress in the role of Scarlett O'Hara. "If we finally wind up with any of the stars that we are testing we must regard ourselves as absolute failures," he wrote to his director, George Cukor, in October 1938.

If Vivien Leigh had not come along, Scarlett would have gone to Paulette Goddard. "She at least has in her favor that she is not stale," Selznick wrote in the same memo.

More than a year earlier, on one of his many trips to Hollywood to work on the script, Sidney Howard wrote his wife that Cukor had already made up his mind about how to cast the movie. Then Howard added, "But I doubt if Selznick ever makes up his."

As late as December 1938—with the movie scheduled to start shooting on January 15—

Left: In this posed studio photograph, a smiling David Selznick (left) and Victor Fleming appear to be going over the script of Gone With the Wind. *The overabundant screenplay had already helped to drive director George Cukor off the movie; when Fleming was hired to replace Cukor, he insisted on a total revision of the script, causing the entire film to be shut down for almost two weeks. Eventually, Fleming would suffer a nervous collapse before the picture was finished. Above: Lyle Wheeler, another USC architecture graduate, dictates notes to his secretary as he examines a model of Atlanta. Two miles of streets were laid on the studio back lot, and the exteriors of fifty-three full-size buildings were constructed.*

Selznick had still not decided who would play three of the four main roles: Scarlett, Ashley Wilkes, and Melanie Hamilton. As to Rhett Butler, Selznick had had his mind made up for him. Goldwyn would not loan out Gary Cooper. Warner would give him Errol Flynn only if he were willing to accept Bette Davis as Scarlett and agreed to release *Gone With the Wind* through Warner Bros. And the American public, or at least the portion of the public that took the time to write to Selznick International Pictures, wanted Clark Gable.

The public was also convinced that the fair-haired, sensitive, British actor Leslie Howard would slip effortlessly into Ashley's Confederate uniform. The only people who disagreed were David Selznick and Leslie Howard.

"All we have to do is line up a complete cast of such people as Hepburn and Leslie Howard, and we can have a lovely picture for release eight years ago," Selznick wrote in a confidential memo to Dan O'Shea, the lawyer who handled contracts for SIP.

At forty-three, Howard thought he was far too old to play the young southern intellectual whom Scarlett pursued for more than a decade. "I'm not nearly beautiful or young enough for Ashley," he wrote to his fourteen-year-old daughter, "and it makes me sick being fixed up to look attractive."

Selznick, too, was worried about Howard's age, and he looked elsewhere. A list of the twenty-six actors to whom Selznick gave "serious consideration" includes Vincent Price, Joel McCrea, Franchot Tone, Ray Milland, and Humphrey Bogart. In the end, it came down to Howard and Melvyn Douglas. Selznick was excited by Douglas's "intelligent reading" but found him "much too beefy physically—suggesting a lieutenant of Rhett Butler's rather than an aesthetic, poetic, and defeated Ashley." Howard, who wanted to be a director and had just starred in and co-directed an excellent screen adaptation of George Bernard Shaw's *Pygmalion*, was enticed into playing Ashley by being offered the position of associate producer on his next movie for Selznick—*Intermezzo*, in which he was to star as the sensitive violinist who has an affair with the actress Selznick had just imported from Sweden, Ingrid Bergman.

"I'm not keen about it," Howard wrote to his daughter before his first screen test for Ashley. "I've never read the book, but I've read the script—miles of it—and I don't know what they're all talking about or what's wrong with them—most of all Ashley. However, money is the mission here, and who am I to refuse it?" Leaving his family behind in England, Howard had come to Hollywood to make money. So, for $75,000, he took the role that he called "the abominable Ashley, a dreadful milk-sop, totally spineless and negative."

As fervently as Howard tried to flee the role of Ashley, Olivia de Havilland pursued the part of Melanie. De Havilland may have been the only young actress who really preferred the sweet, physically frail, but emotionally strong Melanie to the headstrong, morally compromised Scarlett O'Hara. Selznick felt there were a dozen actresses who could play Melanie adequately, but he favored De Havilland after she did a secret reading for him in the drawing room of his house on Summit Drive, with Cukor playing the part of Scarlett.

The audition had to be secret, since De Havilland was owned by another studio. Selznick wished that she were under contract to him or, at least, that she didn't have a contract with Warner Bros. Warners refused to consider loaning De Havilland out, Selznick wrote to O'Shea in November 1938. But Selznick knew that a studio's seeming reluctance to part with a star was often merely a bargaining ploy. There was a two-pronged attack on Warner. De Havilland took Ann Warner, Jack Warner's wife, to tea at the Brown Derby and begged her to intercede, which Ann did; and Selznick turned over to Jack a one-picture commitment he owned on Jimmy Stewart.

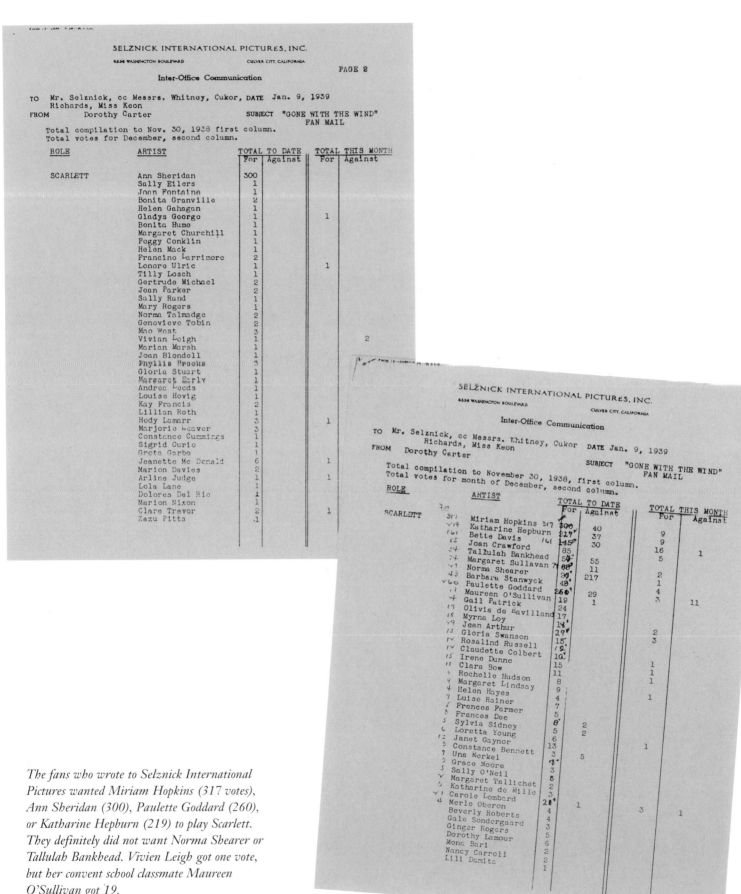

The fans who wrote to Selznick International Pictures wanted Miriam Hopkins (317 votes), Ann Sheridan (300), Paulette Goddard (260), or Katharine Hepburn (219) to play Scarlett. They definitely did not want Norma Shearer or Tallulah Bankhead. Vivien Leigh got one vote, but her convent school classmate Maureen O'Sullivan got 19.

Inter-Office Communication

TO   Mr. Solznick, cc Messrs. Whitney, Cukor   DATE 1/9/39
     Richards, Miss Keon
FROM   Dorothy Carter   SUBJECT "GONE WITH THE WIND"
                                         FAN MAIL

Total compilation to Nov. 30, 1938, first column.
Total votes for December, second column.

ROLE	ARTIST	TOTAL TO DATE For	Against	TOTAL THIS MONTH For	Against
RHETT	Clark Gable	495	166	24	3
	Ronald Colman	61	25	1	
	Basil Rathbone	71	6	5	
	Fredric March	62	13	5	
	Warner Baxter	39			
	Preston Foster	38			
	Melvyn Douglas	27			
	Cary Grant	31	1	1	
	Errol Flynn	26	3		
	Joel McCrea	16			
	Sidney Blackmer	17			
	John Boles	12			
	Richard Dix	12			
	Gary Cooper	17			
	Randolph Scott	9			
	Ricardo Cortez	8			
	Douglas Fairbanks Jr.	7		1	
	John Mack Brown	225			
	Edward Arnold	6		1	
	John Barrymore	5			
	Kent Taylor	3			
	Brian Aherne	3			
	John Miljan	3		1	
	Alan Marshall	4			
	Spencer Tracy	3			
	Warren William	8			
	Walter Pidgeon	10			
	William Powell	12			
	Alan Mowbray	2			
	Caesar Romero	5			
	Robert Taylor	7	1		
	Michael Whalen	4			
	Henry Wilcoxon	2			
	Don Ameche	264			
	Henry Hull	2			
	Cl Henry Gordon	2			
	Victor Jory	2			
	Laurence Olivier	2			
	George Brent	2			
	Nils Asther	2			
	Humphrey Bogart	2			
	Anthony Averill	43			

Inter-Office Communication

TO   Mr. Selznick, cc Messrs. Whitney, Cukor   DATE 1/9/39
     Richards, Miss Keon
FROM   Dorothy Carter   SUBJECT "GONE WITH THE WIND"
                                         FAN MAIL

Total compilation to Nov. 30, 1938, first column.
Total votes for Dec., second column.

ROLE	ARTIST	TOTAL TO DATE For	Against	TOTAL THIS MONTH For	Against
RHETT	Leslie Banks	1			
	Ralph Bellamy	1			
	Charles Bickford	2			
	Charles Boyer	1		1	
	Clive Brook	1			
	John Carradine	1			
	Paul Cavanaugh	1			
	Noel Coward	1			
	Ramon Navarro	1			
	Donald Cook	1			
	Roy D'Arcy	1			
	Robert Donat	1			
	Brian Donlevy	1			
	Douglas Dumbrille	1			
	Ian Hunter	1			
	Jack Holt	1			
	Walter Houston	2			
	Jack LaRue	1			
	Fred MacMurray	1			
	Gilbert Roland	1			
	Victor McLaglen	1			
	Robert Montgomery	1			
	Craig Reynolds	1			
	Onslow Stevens	2			
	James Stewart	1			
	Ray Milland	1			
	Franchot Tone	1			
	Rudy Vallee	1			
	Bruce Cabot	1			
	James Montague	1			
	Paul Muni	1			
	Philip Merrivale	1			
	James Rennie	1			
	Nelson Eddy	1			
	George Sanders	4			
	Nelson Eddy	1			
	George Raft	1			
	Lee Tracey	1			
	Pat O'Brien	1			
	Francis Lederer	1			
	David Niven	1			
	Bryant Washburn	1	5	1	
	Edmund Lowe	1			

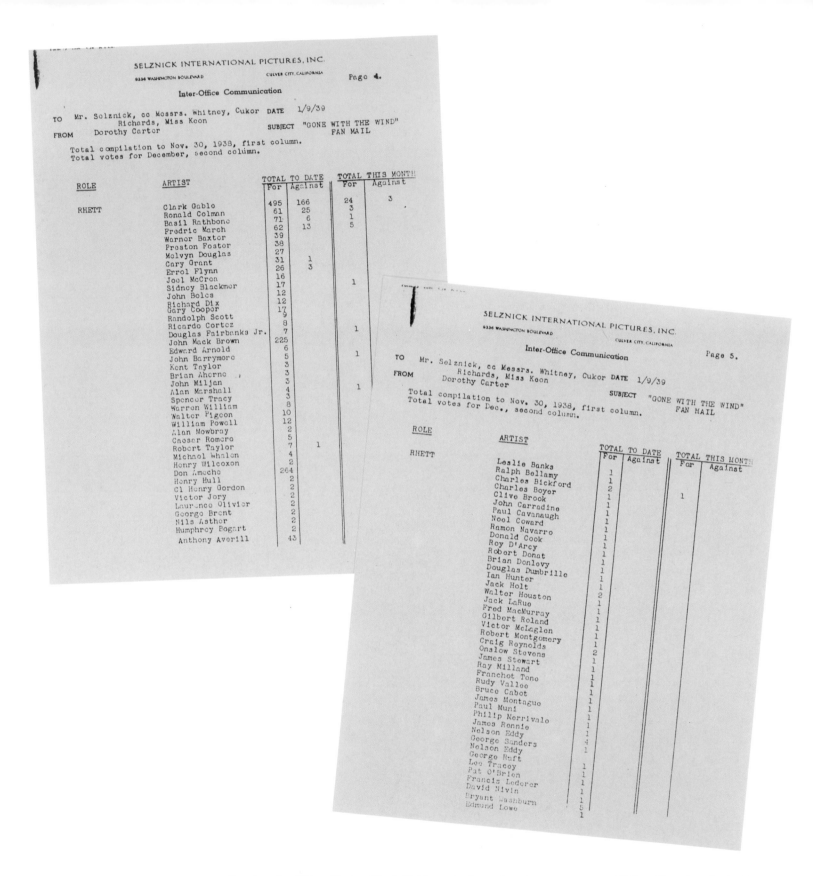

For the role of Rhett Butler, Clark Gable received nearly twice as many votes (495) as Don Ameche (264). Western star Johnny Mack Brown was in third place with 225 votes. Basil Rathbone, who was Margaret Mitchell's personal choice for Rhett, got 71 votes. The studio took such messages from the public seriously. The fan mail was tabulated, and copies were sent to Selznick, studio chairman Jock Whitney, and director Cukor. The 166 votes against Gable may have been part of a campaign by fans who had other favorites.

In January 1939, Olivia de Havilland was twenty-three years old. Vivien Leigh was twenty-six. Clark Gable was thirty-eight, but his age lent weight to the wicked and worldly-wise Captain Butler. Leslie Howard, an intelligent actor, did manage to disguise his forty-three years inside Ashley's well-fitting grey tunic. Over the next five months of rising panic and pressure, the four of them would behave, in many ways, like the characters they portrayed. Or, at least, they would be perceived that way by the other actors and the crew.

Production started on January 26, 1939. Things went wrong from the beginning. Marcella Rabwin, who was Selznick's executive secretary at the time of *Gone With the Wind*, blames the unfinished script: "You cannot go into the making of a five million dollar picture, the most popular book ever written next to the Bible, and be enthusiastic and cooperative and work hard if you don't know what you're going to do in the next five minutes."

But it was more than that. The problem with the motion picture business, in the words of Raymond Klune, the production manager on *Gone With the Wind*, is that "you really make nothing but prototypes. It isn't like making shoes, where you design and make one pair of shoes and then you turn it over to production and make a million pairs just like it."

Selznick had always relied more on instinct and intuition than on blueprints. On the easiest movies, it was a difficult way of working. On *Gone With the Wind*—with its huge budget, enormous cast, and daunting spectacle—it was a recipe for disaster.

"Wardrobe has been unable to make any progress on costumes due to lack of cast to date," assistant director Eric Stacey wrote ten days before the movie started production. At that point, Vivien Leigh had had only one costume fitting; Olivia de Havilland (who was at Warner Bros. finishing *Dodge City*, the fifth movie in which she pined for or was tamed by heroic Errol Flynn) had had no fittings at all. Shooting would start at Tara, but the actors who would play the Tarleton Twins and Scarlett's mother and sisters had not yet been chosen.

"Selznick was a nut for detail," says Evelyn Keyes, who played Scarlett's sister Suellen. But that obsessiveness did not translate into a dependable budget or schedule. Often, Selznick wasn't sure what he wanted until he saw that it was missing. "He went by trial and error," said assistant director Ridgeway Callow. "On *Rebecca*, we shot an insert of a letter nineteen times."

Whenever Selznick had the script of *Gone With the Wind* changed—and it was revised nearly every day during the months before and after the movie started shooting—the sets, set dressings, or camera angles were likely to change with it. A breakdown of scenes to be played in Rhett and Scarlett's Atlanta house in Oliver Garrett's script, for example, had locations that were different from the scenes in Sidney Howard's script. Bonnie's birth was played out in Scarlett's bedroom, the living room, and the lower hall in one script. In the other, the living room was missing, and Mammy told Aunt Pitty about the birth outside the house. Bonnie's death was observed from the rose arbor in one script, through an upstairs window in the other.

"Generally speaking, many of the little mistakes, or mistakes large or little that were made in his operation, grew directly out of his own shortcomings," Klune said of Selznick. "He would be so busy occupied with other things that he would forget or not get around to rewriting a scene that he was dissatisfied with that was scheduled to shoot tomorrow morning. And it was not at all unlikely for him to call me up at home at two o'clock in the morning and ask me to change the next morning's call or schedule. Those things were not done without cost or confusion."

Nor were they without cost to Selznick. The harsh penalty he would pay when he needed more money to complete *Gone With the Wind* was the eventual loss of his studio.

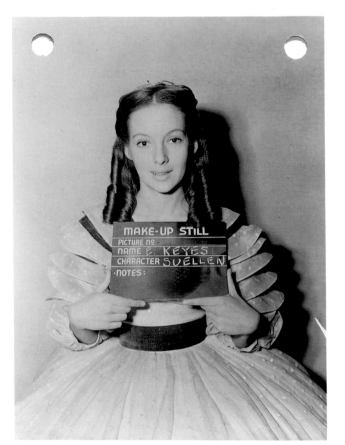

Above left: Selznick was afraid that nineteen-year-old Evelyn Keyes might look "dangerously young" next to Vivien Leigh, who was twenty-six. Keyes, who was under contract to Cecil B. De Mille, came from Atlanta. "The first time I met De Mille," says Keyes, "he pointed his finger at me and said, 'That accent has to go.' So I took diction lessons. Then I was sent over for Gone With the Wind, and I had to relearn the accent." Above right: Ann Rutherford was best known as Andy Hardy's girlfriend, Polly Benedict, in a series of M-G-M movies starring Mickey Rooney.

By January 26, 1939, at 8:00 A.M. when Vivien Leigh, Hattie McDaniel, and George Reeves and Fred Crane as the Tarleton brothers set foot on the Forty Acres, $869,000 had already been spent on *Gone With the Wind*. George Cukor, who joined them there on the porch of Tara, had been paid approximately $240,000 of that pre-production money, and $159,000 had gone toward studio overhead.

Cukor was Selznick's favorite director. When Selznick first ran a studio, RKO, Cukor discovered Katharine Hepburn for him and in one year, 1932, directed four of his pictures—*What Price Hollywood?*, *A Bill of Divorcement*, *Rockabye*, and *Our Betters*. In 1933, Selznick took Cukor with him to M-G-M where he produced and Cukor directed *Dinner At Eight* in 1933 and *David Copperfield* in 1935. However, by the time that *Gone With the Wind* started shooting, Selznick was beginning to feel desperate about money, and, although it was his own fault that the production had been delayed, he resented the fact that he had been paying Cukor $4,000 a week to do casting searches and screen tests. Selznick was particularly annoyed that Cukor, who was finicky about the movies he directed, had turned down *A Star Is Born* and *Tom Sawyer* and was unwilling to direct *Intermezzo*. A case could be made that Selznick's resentment was one of the triggers that caused him to fire Cukor after just fourteen days of shooting.

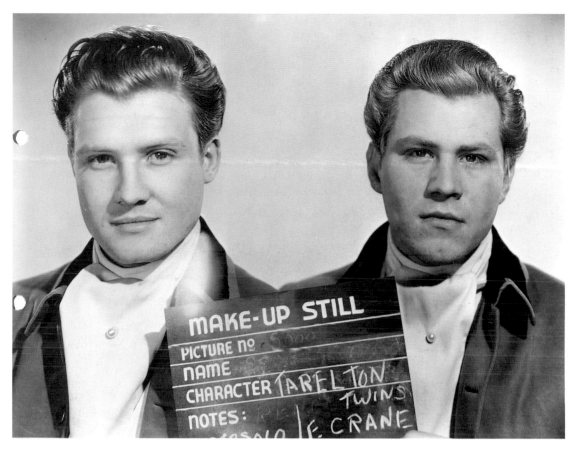

George Bessolo (left) changed his name to George Reeves during the filming of Gone With the Wind. *From 1951 to 1957, Reeves starred as the television incarnation of the comic-book hero in the syndicated* Adventures of Superman. *He committed suicide in 1959. Fred Crane played Brent Tarleton, but the screen credits listed him as Stuart. According to Crane, it took eight hours to dye his hair the bright carrot-top of the Tarleton Twins. Since the two actors still did not look enough alike, the Tarleton Twins were changed to the Tarleton brothers.*

Much of Cukor's work was reshot by Victor Fleming, but Cukor's influence on the film was not erased as easily. His eye and sensibility had helped to shape the costumes and the sets. Most of *Gone With the Wind* was not shot in continuity because Rhett Butler had a relatively small number of scenes, occurring years apart, and it would have cost too much to have an important star on salary throughout endless scenes between Scarlett and Melanie. But Cukor had insisted on shooting in continuity for the first few weeks to allow his actors to discover their characters. Although only 5 percent of the finished movie is Cukor's work, he is in large part responsible for the performances of Vivien Leigh and Olivia de Havilland, not least because both actresses came to his house for private coaching throughout the months of production.

The announcement that Cukor would leave *Gone With the Wind* was made on February 13. David—carelessly cruel and carefully kind—had already made sure that Cukor had a more suitable job, directing M-G-M's *The Women*. Cukor has often been derided as a "woman's director," with the unspoken subtext that no homosexual can adequately direct men. To prove that premise false, one has only to rent two videos and watch Lew Ayres and Cary Grant in *Holiday*, and James Stewart and Cary Grant in *The Philadelphia Story*. But Cukor was at his best in the parlor and bedroom. He was not a director of flamboyant action, and Selznick always intended to have William Cameron Menzies direct the big action sequences in *Gone With the Wind*.

After Vivien Leigh was chosen, the press complained that Scarlett was a role for an American girl;
Selznick responded that Scarlett's background was French and Irish and so was Vivien Leigh's.
Leigh was born in India on November 5, 1913. Like most children of civil servants toiling around the
Empire, Leigh was sent to England to be educated. She left India at the age of six and didn't see her mother
again for two years. (A scene from Gone With the Wind © *1939 Turner Entertainment Co.*
All Rights Reserved. Photo: Photofest)

Cukor's friendship with Selznick was barely tarnished. That was the odd thing about David. Almost no one he fired took it personally once the first sting of humiliation was over. Somehow, David's enthusiasm and the way he excited and encouraged everyone who worked for him made him too likable to hate. Even Sidney Howard admitted, grudgingly, that he liked Selznick better than Goldwyn. Lee Garmes, Cukor's *Gone With the Wind* cinematographer, was also fired by Selznick, yet he came back to photograph *Duel in the Sun* for him. And Cukor gradually began to wear his dismissal as a badge of honor. Whenever a distinguished director was removed from a film, Cukor would telephone and say: "Now look here, I'm going to tell you something that may be of some encouragement to you. I was put off the *biggest* picture ever made, and I'm here to tell the tale."

Gone With the Wind was shut down for twelve days in February to change directors and let Ben Hecht take a stab at the script. Those twelve days were the last vacation some of the actors—Vivien Leigh, most of all—would have for four months.

Above: Scarlett is surrounded by admirers. In his notes, Menzies wrote that he was trying to get "sunshiny effects" at the barbecue: "The silhouette f.g. from where Ashley & Melanie observe the barbeque brings out the sunshine & gay costumes beyond. For contrast the next time we see Twelve Oaks it was in ruins & in the steely blue grey of dawn." Below: An early, unsigned, four-segmented storyboard of the barbecue at Twelve Oaks in which Scarlett looks nothing like Mitchell's character and the Tarleton Twins can be recognized by their orange hair.

M arch was a new beginning. Victor Fleming had been directing movies since 1920, learning his craft on silent films like *Law of the Lawless* and *Call of the Canyon*. Eight years before that, in 1912, he had lucked his way into movies when he fixed a broken camera for a fly-by-night movie crew and was hired as their cameraman. Fleming's reputation as a man's man was no publicity stunt. He flew a plane, rode an Ariel Square Four twenty years before motorcycles were fashionable, and shot innumerable wildcats in the hills above his Bel Air home, laying the carcasses in front of his bedroom door. His daughter, Victoria, describes him as "a blend of General George Patton and General Douglas MacArthur."

No other director has ever received screen credit for two pictures as memorable and long lasting as *Gone With the Wind* and *The Wizard of Oz* in the same year, but Fleming did not see himself as the general in charge of *Gone With the Wind*. It was Fleming's job to give Selznick what he wanted, and Fleming did it as quickly, forcefully, and economically as he could. There is irony in the fact that while Cukor genuinely liked David and Fleming was contemptuous of David's disorganization and indecision, it is Fleming who shaped the movie to Selznick's will without too much fuss.

Although Fleming received the screen credit for directing *Gone With the Wind*, he shot, at most, 55 percent of the movie. (Ray Rennahan, the cameraman sent by Technicolor, thought Fleming directed no more than 45 percent of the film.) William Cameron Menzies was responsible for some montages, the fire sequence, and many of the big scenes in Atlanta during the war, including the grim citizens dreading the casualty lists from the battle of Gettysburg and Scarlett's harrowing journey through the streets. Sam Wood, who took Fleming's place for two weeks in May and who then shot side by side with Fleming for another three weeks, filmed the story of Scarlett and her second husband, Frank Kennedy; the scenes surrounding the birth of Bonnie Blue Butler; and many of the postwar scenes between Scarlett and Ashley. And Cukor's sequences of Scarlett and Mammy preparing for the barbecue, Melanie's childbirth, Scarlett and Melanie killing and disposing of the Union cavalryman, and Rhett bringing Scarlett the Paris hat remained in the film.

Fleming began shooting on March 2 and—except for creating the barbecue at Twelve Oaks—spent most of the month retaking scenes that Cukor had already filmed. In February, Selznick had sent a blistering memo about the "very cheap, ordinary and thoughtless costuming job" on the extras in the Bazaar sequence where Rhett pays $150 in gold to dance with Scarlett; and he was delighted by the opportunity to film the dance again.

He was less delighted by the expense. The twelve days of idle time had wasted more than $30,000 in salaries and overhead. The revised script by Ben Hecht meant $35,000 in new sets. The retakes meant more extras, $885 worth of costumes for the extras, $1,588 in props and live-stock to dress the sets, $2,073 worth of lighting supplies and an additional $1,781 to pay the grips and electricians who struggled with the lights. Ominously, by March 20, the movie was already six days behind schedule, and the estimated final budget was $300,000 higher than it had been a month earlier.

As always, David defended himself against anxiety with words. To another Hollywood prince, novelist Budd Schulberg, Selznick's 5,000-word memos "were a natural extension of the verbal Niagara that poured from him day and night, for he was also a nocturnal force who seemed unable to stop the flow until he fell asleep from exhaustion in the early hours. Later, when I heard about Thomas Wolfe . . . the prodigious novelist reminded me of a literary ver-

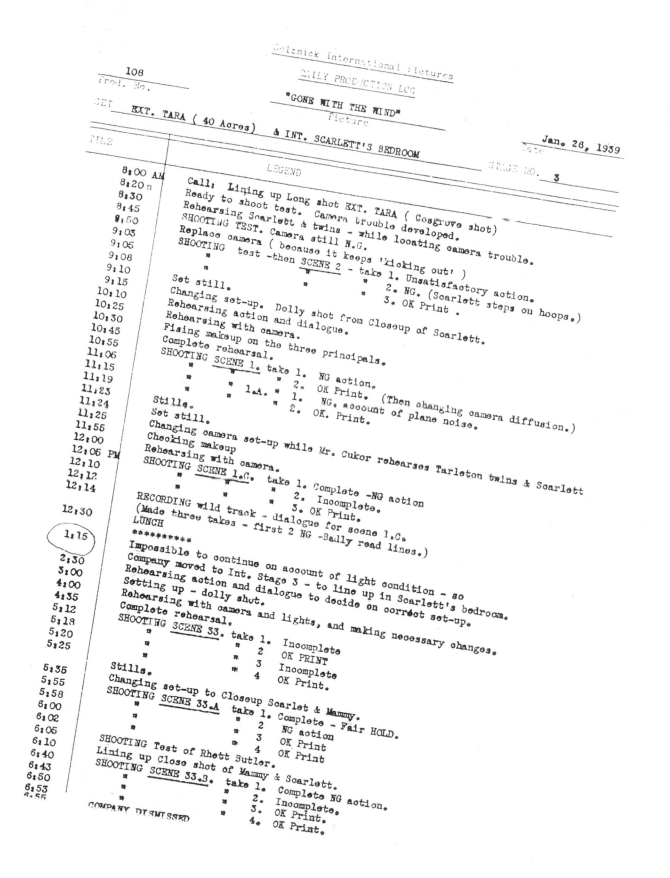

108
Prod. No.

"GONE WITH THE WIND"
Picture

SET   EXT. TARA (40 Acres)   & INT. SCARLETT'S BEDROOM

Jan. 26, 1939
Date

FILE

STAGE NO.   3

LEGEND

Time	
8:00 AM	Call: Lining up Long shot EXT. TARA (Cosgrove shot)
8:20 n	Ready to shoot test. Camera trouble developed.
8:30	Rehearsing Scarlett & twins - while locating camera trouble.
8:45	SHOOTING TEST. Camera still N.G.
9:50	Replace camera (because it keeps 'kicking out!')
9:03	SHOOTING test -then SCENE 2 - take 1. Unsatisfactory action.
9:05	" 2. NG. (Scarlett steps on hoops.)
9:08	" 3. OK Print .
9:10	Set still.
9:15	Changing set-up. Dolly shot from Closeup of Scarlett.
10:10	Rehearsing action and dialogue.
10:25	Rehearsing with camera.
10:30	Fixing makeup on the three principals.
10:45	Complete rehearsal.
10:55	SHOOTING SCENE 1. take 1. NG action.
11:06	" 2. OK Print. (Then changing camera diffusion.)
11:15	" 1.A. " 1. NG. account of plane noise.
11:19	" 2. OK. Print.
11:23	Stills.
11:24	Set still.
11:25	Changing camera set-up while Mr. Cukor rehearses Tarleton twins & Scarlett
11:55	Checking makeup
12:00	Rehearsing with camera.
12:05 PM	SHOOTING SCENE 1.C. take 1. Complete -NG action
12:10	" 2. Incomplete.
12:12	" 3. OK Print.
12:14	RECORDING wild track - dialogue for scene 1.C.
12:30	(Made three takes - first 2 NG -Badly read lines.)
1:15	LUNCH *********
2:30	Impossible to continue on account of light condition - so
3:00	Company moved to Int. Stage 3 - to line up in Scarlett's bedroom.
4:00	Rehearsing action and dialogue to decide on correct set-up.
4:35	Setting up - dolly shot.
5:12	Rehearsing with camera and lights, and making necessary changes.
5:18	Complete rehearsal.
5:20	SHOOTING SCENE 33. take 1. Incomplete
5:25	" 2 OK PRINT
	" 3 Incomplete
	" 4 OK Print.
5:35	Stills.
5:55	Changing set-up to Closeup Scarlet & Mammy.
5:58	SHOOTING SCENE 33.A take 1. Complete - Fair HOLD.
6:00	" 2 Complete
6:02	" 3 NG action
6:05	" 4 OK Print
6:10	SHOOTING Test of Rhett Butler.
6:40	Lining up Close shot of Mammy & Scarlett.
6:43	SHOOTING SCENE 33.B. take 1. Complete NG action.
6:50	" 2. Incomplete.
6:53	" 3. OK Print.
6:55	" 4. OK Print.
	COMPANY DISMISSED

The company worked from 8:00 A.M. to 6:55 P.M. on January 26, 1939, the first day of production.
During the next six months, it was not uncommon to work long after 7:00 P.M., and often until midnight.

Above: While Vivien Leigh had a rapport with sympathetic director George Cukor, Clark Gable felt isolated at a strange studio (The Fred A. Parrish Collection). To make matters worse, Gable, who was not comfortable on a dance floor, tried and failed to learn the Virginia Reel for his first scenes. A special camera dolly was then built to give the illusion that Rhett and Scarlett were dancing. Facing page: Walter Plunkett dresses the dance-scene extras (The Fred A. Parrish Collection). The wardrobe department created hundreds of hoop skirts.

sion of David Selznick, larger than life and pouring words from a bottomless well, good words, great words, needless words all gushing forth together, flooding one's mind."

The words began to turn ugly. In a useless memo sent on March 11 to Fleming, Menzies, costume designer Walter Plunkett, and five other technicians including his art director and set decorator, Selznick lauded the realistic look of French movies and complained: "I feel that our sets always look exactly what they are—sets that have been put up a few hours before. . . . The same is true of the costumes. They always look exactly what they are—fresh out of the Costume Department, instead of looking like clothes that have been worn."

Ray Klune, one of the people to whom that memo was directed, would walk out on Selznick four years later when the memos got too much to bear. After *Since You Went Away*, David sent Klune, who was hospitalized with pneumonia, a three-page letter in which, said Klune, "He went all back through *Since You Went Away* and retraced mistakes which he was seemingly trying to lay at my door. Most of the mistakes that were made were of his own making, in a strange kind of way, because David never stuck to his own job. He was always kind of neglecting his own job and getting into other peoples' jobs. And we told him that time and again, that he could do any one of those jobs better than the person doing it. The person doing those jobs, however, couldn't do what he should be doing, which was producing."

Klune resigned. The next day he accepted an offer from Darryl Zanuck at 20th Century-Fox. Klune thought Selznick and Zanuck were equally creative, but Zanuck, who knew how to delegate, "let people do their jobs;" and Klune stayed with him for thirteen years. Yet Klune couldn't remain angry with Selznick, "a wonderful strange kind of fellow" who apologized abjectly for sending the letter and offered to triple Klune's salary if he would stay.

F. Scott Fitzgerald wrote of his hero in *The Last Tycoon* that Monroe Stahr could keep the whole equation of movies in his head. Stahr was based on Irving Thalberg; clumsy, passionate, word-drunk David Selznick who was always stumbling over the foot in his mouth and then apologizing had none of Stahr's coolness and elegance. But, in his uncontrolled way, David embraced the equation, even if his solution was marred by blots and erasures and second guesses. He was every bit as good as Thalberg at remaking movies in the editing room, and he was a genius at casting. He had taste, an instinct for what audiences wanted to see, and, for a time, the rare ability to mix good taste with good box office. If he had had any self-discipline at all, no one would have equaled him.

But as March lurched into April, *Gone With the Wind* spun out of control. There was no one to impose discipline on Selznick, no one to play the role of superego the way his father-in-law, L. B. Mayer, did during David's years at M-G-M. He was working fourteen hours a day, keeping himself awake with thyroid pills and Benzedrine, while he tried to oversee every detail of *Gone With the Wind* and also to prepare *Rebecca* which would start production in the summer. "Selznick was a very hard worker," said Hal Kern, who was cutting *Gone With the Wind* together as each sequence was shot. "He also played hard. He burnt the candle at both ends."

The Bazaar in the autumn of 1862 was held to benefit Atlanta's military hospital. Within the year, that hospital would overflow with dying soldiers.

"*INT. BAZAAR — LONG SHOT*
The great armory drill room is decorated for
the occasion. Around the walls are little
booths with pretty Atlanta girls in attendance
on their customers. The floor is filled with
dancers in bright evening dresses. . . . The
room is lit by candles in donated candlesticks.
The walls are decorated with flag bunting,
and ivy vines."
Gone With the Wind *screenplay*

To relieve the pressure, Selznick gambled, smoked four packs of cigarettes a day, pursued the typists and aspiring actresses who showed up at his office, and wrote more and more memos. Many of the memos were brilliant. It was Selznick who caught the error when Thomas Mitchell as Gerald O'Hara said, "After we fire on the Yankees at Fort Sumpter." The Confederates had shelled Fort Sumpter before that scene at Twelve Oaks. And Selznick had already begun to shape the actors' performances in the editing room. "It seems to me that we are too far away from Scarlett when she leaves Rhett in the library and runs to the stairs," one memo begins. "We miss her emotion during this moment and it has the additional disadvantage of making her tears, when we finally do come to her . . . something of a shock." But the torrent of memos made the crew edgy; the new dialogue that Selznick would write at night and send down to the sound stages in the morning made most of the actors surly.

As much as possible, the script supervisor, Barbara Keon, tried not to send the pink and blue pages that meant a scene had been rewritten. "I am <u>not</u> sending out pink pages, because they are simple changes, and Mr. Fleming mentioned today that pink pages scare the actors," Keon wrote on March 8. David's changes that day for the scenes at Twelve Oaks included:

```
Scene 56, Page 25: Ashley's line, change to:
"It's so unaware that it may not last forever." (instead of "It's so
unconscious...")

Scene 66, Page 31: Ashley's speech should read:
"Now please—don't go tweaking his nose any more—You may be needed for
more important fighting, Charles. And, after all, Mr. Butler is our guest.
If you'll excuse me, I'll show him around."
```

Keon added, "For God's sake, please see that changes are written in Ashley's script <u>ahead</u> of time."

It wasn't that Leslie Howard couldn't learn his lines. He simply hated Ashley. He also hated the script which he described to his son as, "Just one climax after another . . . full of deaths and murders and passions and jealousies and fighting—oh, and fires, lots of Technicolor fires"; and he wasn't too fond of Hollywood "which now seems to me to resemble a vast village of gaudily painted mud huts inhabited by a huge tribe of pleasant but very, very primitive aborigines."

It was Howard's badge of honor not to read the novel, no matter how many copies Selznick sent him and no matter how much Selznick pleaded. However, he did study his script less sloth-fully after he was dressed down by Vivien Leigh for not knowing his lines. Howard had never met Leigh in England, although he had seen her on the stage and wanted her to play Ophelia to his Hamlet. In Hollywood, he heard her voice before he saw her. He had just finished a test for Ashley when he heard what he described as "the most terrific Southern accent on the next set." It was Leigh testing for Scarlett; she had created the accent in less than a week.

Leigh never had trouble with her lines. Like Scarlett, she was singleminded. "They were handing her new scenes every day," says Evelyn Keyes. "The first script is white, the next rewrite pink, the next one blue. There was no white paper left in the *Gone With the Wind* script. I would watch this woman look at the new pages—I swear, only once—and then go right into being Scarlett O'Hara. She would be standing right there with the paper that had just been handed to her. And she was wonderful."

What the actors remember best nearly sixty years later is the unfinished script. "Pieces came down in all colors," says Rand Brooks, who was on salary for four months but worked only seventeen days as Scarlett's first husband, Charles Hamilton. "Vivien was the hardest working

In an interview with the BBC, film editor Hal Kern (above) said that Gone With the Wind *was photographed, edited, previewed, and ready for release more quickly than any other movie during his sixteen years with Selznick because there simply wasn't time for Selznick to spend his usual seven or eight months editing (The Fred A. Parrish Collection). Today, by comparison, vast editing staffs are engaged to cut pictures half as long in twice the amount of time. The fact that Kern and two assistants edited the film as quickly as they did is nothing less than remarkable. Selznick was so pleased with Kern's work that he gave him an eight-week vacation with pay.*

lady I've met in my whole life." Brooks remembers Howard handling the script changes more defiantly: "As Leslie Howard did the pages, he crumpled them up and threw them away."

Gable was Gable. A great movie star who lacked confidence in his ability as an actor, Gable had been ordered to play Rhett Butler by M-G-M. He never wanted the role, and he refused to use a southern accent. His Rhett Butler came from Ohio, not Charleston. Yet Gable's lack of an accent made Rhett—appropriately—seem even more of an outsider.

At this distance and with the filming of the movie encrusted with mythology, it is hard to say how large a part Gable played in getting Cukor fired. At the very least, he complained about Cukor and was more comfortable with his motorcycle buddy, Victor Fleming, who shot almost all of the scenes involving Gable. But Gable was never really comfortable with the role or the studio. He was slow at learning lines, and the constant dialogue changes upset him. In addition, he had an extremely large neck, and his costumes didn't fit until Selznick hired Gable's private tailor to redo the collars. Nor did he have the rapport with the crew that he was said to have had at M-G-M. "He was very aloof," said assistant director Callow, who tells a story about Gable playing a joke on Hattie McDaniel by putting real Scotch in her pretend Sherry during the scene where Rhett offers Mammy a drink. It was the last shot of the day, and Callow suggested that Gable leave the bottle for the crew. Gable refused and gave the Scotch to his make-up man to take back to his dressing room.

Leslie Howard was more of a gentleman, frequently inviting Callow to share a bottle of wine and a luncheon basket that had been packed by his "secretary." Howard, in his quiet way, was much more of a womanizer than Gable. It was sometimes said that Gable's best job of acting was his imitation in real life of Fleming's man's man persona.

The problems of March were only a prelude to the problems of April. When Sidney Howard returned for two weeks in April—Selznick cajoled the writer into staying for the entire month—the vessel was already scraping against the reef. "How really astonishing that a man can spend the time and money he has spent and find himself so unready at the end," Howard wrote of Selznick. "And he is as completely unready as though he had barely started."

Howard was shown the sequences that Hal Kern had already cut together and was bitterly disappointed. "I thought the stuff beautiful in color, dull, and cold in action," Howard wrote his wife. "Leigh quite extraordinarily fine as Scarlett though not really an actress of much accomplishment. Gable simply terrible as Rhett, awkward, hick, unconvincing." When Howard questioned Victor Fleming about why certain emotionally important scenes had been dropped—including Rhett's return of Melanie's wedding ring—Fleming responded that "the screen is no place for trivial character."

During April, writing was the easier half of Sidney Howard's job. He was also forced into the role of psychiatrist to David and to the crew: "I have never been placed in quite this position of having everybody come to me to take their troubles to David because I am the only person around who doesn't upset him. And he feels that and calls me in to listen to all manner of problems with which, as a writer, I have nothing whatever to do." David was doubled over with chronic indigestion, Fleming was living on stimulants during the day and sedatives at night, and "half the staff look, talk and behave as though they were on the verge of breakdowns," Howard wrote his wife.

Ray Klune avoided a breakdown, although, he said, "At the end of the day, going home, I would be so exhausted, that I would actually cry from sheer exhaustion."

Fleming wasn't as lucky. On Saturday, April 29, after two difficult days of shooting Melanie's death, Fleming stormed off the set and didn't return for two weeks. Selznick, who always lived near the emotional edge, had seen Fleming's breakdown coming. He warned O'Shea on April 14 that Fleming was "so near the breaking point both physically and mentally from sheer exhaustion that it would be a miracle, in my opinion, if he is able to shoot for another seven or eight weeks." Although Marcella Rabwin thought Fleming left partly out of spite, Olivia de Havilland had been shocked a week or so earlier when Fleming confided that he had contemplated suicide the previous Saturday night. And Fleming later told his friend John Lee Mahin that, driving home to Malibu, he had seriously considered driving his car over a cliff.

May was the nightmare month. By May 1, Selznick was secretly and unsuccessfully trying to buy more health and disability insurance on Vivien Leigh.

In 1939, actors and crew worked six days a week, and Scarlett was in nearly every scene of *Gone With the Wind*. The call sheets show that between March 2, when Victor Fleming took over, and June 27, Vivien had exactly three days off, excluding Sundays. She was free on Sundays until June when Selznick began shooting seven days a week. Clark Gable's contract allowed him to go home at 6:00 P.M. every day, and he never waived that right. Vivien was in makeup at 7:00 A.M. and often worked until midnight. It was a schedule that would have destroyed most actors, and Vivien was frail with weak lungs. But she was relentless—never showing exhaustion, never blowing her lines, always willing to do a scene again and then again. One night it was so cold that the horses kept ruining the scene by urinating on camera. "It happened fourteen times," said Callow, "and Vivien never complained. . . . Another time when she was hiding from the cavalry—remember, underneath the bridge—we dirtied her up and she said, 'Oh, I'm not dirty enough.' Then she threw herself in the mud and rolled in it."

One reason Selznick had been reluctant to give the role of Scarlett to Paulette Goddard was because Goddard was living with Charlie Chaplin, presumably without benefit of matrimony. He had chosen, instead, a highly sexed, complicated woman who was passionately in love with a married man.

In the world of the double standard, men were allowed to be men. (It was only after finishing retakes for the Bazaar sequence at the end of March that Gable had legitimized his affair with Carole Lombard by eloping to Arizona.) Women, however, were required to be ladies—on screen as well as off. One of the problems Selznick had with Joe Breen and the Production Code was Scarlett's obvious delight in having been ravished by Rhett. Selznick's story editor Val Lewton said Breen felt the morning after scene "too patently states that Scarlett enjoyed the rape and is now lying in bed figuratively licking her chops." Being a lady was no problem for Olivia de Havilland, who was involved in a platonic relationship with Howard Hughes. It was a great problem for Vivien Leigh, whose sexual passions served as an anti-depressant.

Selznick provided his star with a level headed secretary, Sunny Lash, who was always able to lie convincingly when she told telephone callers that Laurence Olivier was not at Vivien's house. "David wanted his Scarlett to be the perfect little virgin Southern Belle," said Lash. "And nothing should tarnish her character, so he put twenty-four hour guard service around her house so that no one could come near her to try and take pictures of Larry coming in or coming out."

After Olivier went to New York to star with Katharine Cornell in S. N. Behrman's play, *No Time For Comedy*, Selznick defused Vivien's growing tension by flying Olivier west and Vivien east to Kansas City for a weekend. They met in a hotel lobby and, according to Vivien, spent the entire weekend in bed.

It has been said that Vivien was eager to get the movie finished so she could get back in the arms of Olivier. But her relentlessness was more than that. At seven, sent from India to convent school in England, she had told her nine-year-old classmate Maureen O'Sullivan, "When I leave school, I'm going to be a great actress." She had fallen in love with Olivier's talent as well as his body, and she wanted to be worthy of him.

Anyone who reads a biography of Vivien Leigh cannot fail to see a perfect match of actress and role. Like Scarlett, Vivien was impulsive, practical, shrewd, and quick-witted without being intellectual, a Catholic to whom religion meant little, prone to sudden romantic attachments, and ruthless in pursuit of the things or people she wanted. When she was eighteen and saw thirty-one-year-old Leigh Holman on horseback, she said, "I think he looks the perfect Englishman. I'm going to marry him." And she did. When she pursued Olivier and Scarlett to Hollywood, she left her five-year-old daughter behind in England without a backward glance.

Memories of Vivien Leigh are mixed. To film editor Hal Kern, Vivien "was the bitch she was in the picture." When it was time for her daily telephone call to Olivier, everything else had to wait, said Kern, including the production of *Gone With the Wind*. But, to Ridgeway Callow, "she was a real pro." "She never stopped working," says Evelyn Keyes, who was slapped so hard by Vivien in one scene that the imprint of Vivien's hand stayed on her cheek for hours.

To Ann Rutherford, who played Scarlett's youngest sister Carreen, "She hurled herself at everything. She burned herself, she was such a hard worker. We watched her lose weight. In a break she'd take her costume off and the wardrobe girls would put more seams in what once had been a tightly fitted dress." Rutherford was a friend of George Cukor's. "Before important scenes, Vivien would drive to George's house on Cordell and George would give her what he called a nursery dinner—lamb chop, baked potato, something very simple—and they'd go over tomorrow's scenes," says Rutherford, who remembers Vivien staggering into Cukor's house "more dead than alive."

On the call sheets for Monday, May 1, Sam Wood is listed as the director of *Gone With the Wind*. After Fleming's collapse two days earlier, Selznick had borrowed Wood from M-G-M. Wood was a competent director, but he was considerably less stormy and robust than Victor Fleming, so Vivien had an easier time during the first few weeks of May. Fleming had bullied and harrassed her, partly because he was sadistic to actresses (when Fleming got married he ordered the justice of the peace to leave the word "love" out of the ceremony) and partly to turn her Scarlett into a bitter and tough woman.

Sidney Howard left at the beginning of May, but Selznick continued rewriting the dialogue. New script pages were sent to the set on May 1, 2, 11, 12, 15, 16, 17, 18, 23, 25, 26, and 27. The final script, boxed in the Selznick Archive, is a rainbow of white, pink, blue, yellow, and green pages, demonstrating that some scenes were written, and presumably given to the actors to play, five times.

Through it all, Olivia de Havilland was kind and uncomplaining. "She was a sweetheart. She would do anything that you asked of her," said Hal Kern. Olivia even volunteered to record Scarlett's retching after Vivien Leigh refused to belch for the scene in which Scarlett gets sick eating radishes. Much as Melanie fussed over Scarlett, Olivia worried when she returned from a four-week hiatus and found Vivien so shockingly thin that she passed her without recognizing her.

Fleming returned in mid-May. It was then that the most terrible crisis on *Gone With the Wind* occurred. Selznick ran out of money.

David went to his father-in-law at M-G-M. But family was family, and business was business, and while L. B. admired David, he had never much liked him. To finance the rest of the movie, M-G-M demanded the unacceptable—total ownership of *Gone With the Wind*. When M-G-M refused to help him and all the Whitneys except Jock deserted him, David threw the dice bravely and, to secure a loan from the Bank of America, mortgaged his stake in *Gone With the Wind*, *Rebecca*, and *Intermezzo*. It was Jock who secured the $2,050,000 loan for David. In return for $1 million to complete *Gone With the Wind* and enough money to make the other two movies, the bankrupt Selznick International Pictures was at the mercy of the Whitneys and of their lawyer, John Wharton. Wharton—who loved the theater and admired Sidney Howard immensely—was implacably antagonistic toward Selznick, not only because of his waste of the Whitneys' money but also because Wharton felt that David lacked character. A year later Wharton was the lead executioner of SIP.[4]

With the money in hand, Selznick could think of nothing but finishing *Gone With the Wind*. Sometime during the two-and-a-half-years of incubation, *Gone With the Wind* had become more than just another movie. As fervently as Ahab had pursued his whale, David pursued some vision of the greatest and the best. So the nightmare of May turned into the fever dream of June. One has only to look at the call sheets and daily production logs to read the hysteria beneath the flat, declarative sentences.

---

4. Wharton helped Sidney Howard, Robert Sherwood, and three other major playwrights form the Playwrights Producing Company. In his book, *Life Among the Playwrights*, he contrasted Howard, who had returned a non-refundable $500 advance when he felt he could not make a worthwhile play from the book he was asked to adapt, with Selznick, whose profligacy appalled him.

"*Mr. Westmore is working with Miss Leigh today on various hair styles, eyebrow and lip makeup for Mr. Cukor's approval. Mr. Cukor suggests that photographs of these be made in the Photo Gallery this afternoon.*"
Memo from assistant director Eric Stacey, January 16, 1939

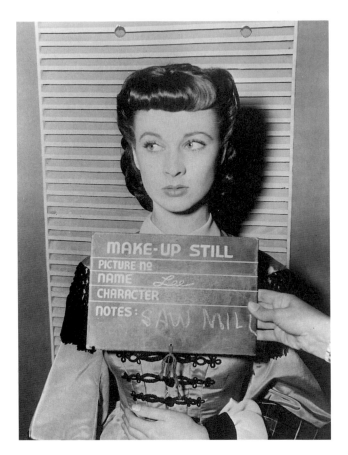

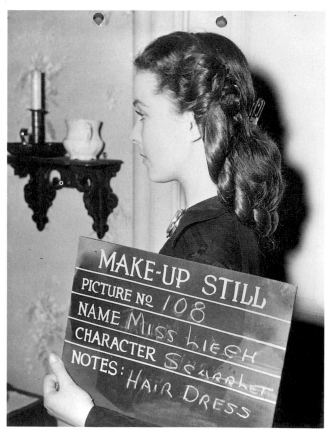

If proof is needed that Vivien Leigh was not a star in January 1939, note the misspelling of her name in this set of hair and makeup stills.

Right: Vivien Leigh poses with Mozelle Miller, her stand-in and double (Collection Dennis A. Shaw and James Tumblin). Facing page: An exhausted Leigh, who has been up since 2:00 A.M., slumps in her dressing room after Scarlett's "I'll never be hungry again" speech (The Fred A. Parrish Collection).

On Saturday, June 3, Vivien Leigh had an 8:00 A.M. makeup call and spent the day shooting scenes with Clark Gable in the summer of 1872 for Victor Fleming. At 7:00 P.M. she shifted to Sam Wood and spent the evening doing process shots against a background projected on a screen. On June 7, Scarlett was abandoned by Rhett Butler in the autumn of 1872 all day under Fleming's direction. At 6:00 P.M. she was back at Tara mixing soap for Wood and trying to survive during the early days of Reconstruction.

The script was revised on June 2, 3, 5, 7, 8, 9, 10, 17, 20, 22, and 23. On June 8, Selznick was on the set writing dialogue for a scene between Rhett and Scarlett; the first shot of the day didn't take place until 2:18 P.M. For five nights in late May and early June, Leigh had a 2:00 A.M. call to shoot the dawn scenes of Scarlett's savage defiance of fate that ended the movie's first half. Four times the pre-dawn wait was fruitless because the sunrise was not properly glorious. On June 26, the day before she finished working, Vivien began the day as a sixteen-year-old girl in a pretty white dress flirting with the Tarleton boys on the porch of Tara. That was followed by spring, 1866; summer, 1872; a scene at the Twelve Oaks barbecue in 1861; and Atlanta in the summer of 1864.

The production logs show how close they all were to breaking down at the end. On June 1, Fleming suddenly decided that the set of Bonnie's bedroom, with the child's body laid out on the bed, was wrong, although he had approved it the night before. Fleming spent two hours rearranging furniture; when the furniture was in position, someone spilled a paint pot on the rug, and everyone waited while a fresh carpet was laid. On June 22, Fleming took a sudden dislike to the dishes and silver at Rhett's table in the New Orleans Cafe and demanded that the table appointments be changed. That day the cameras first rolled at 3:56 P.M.

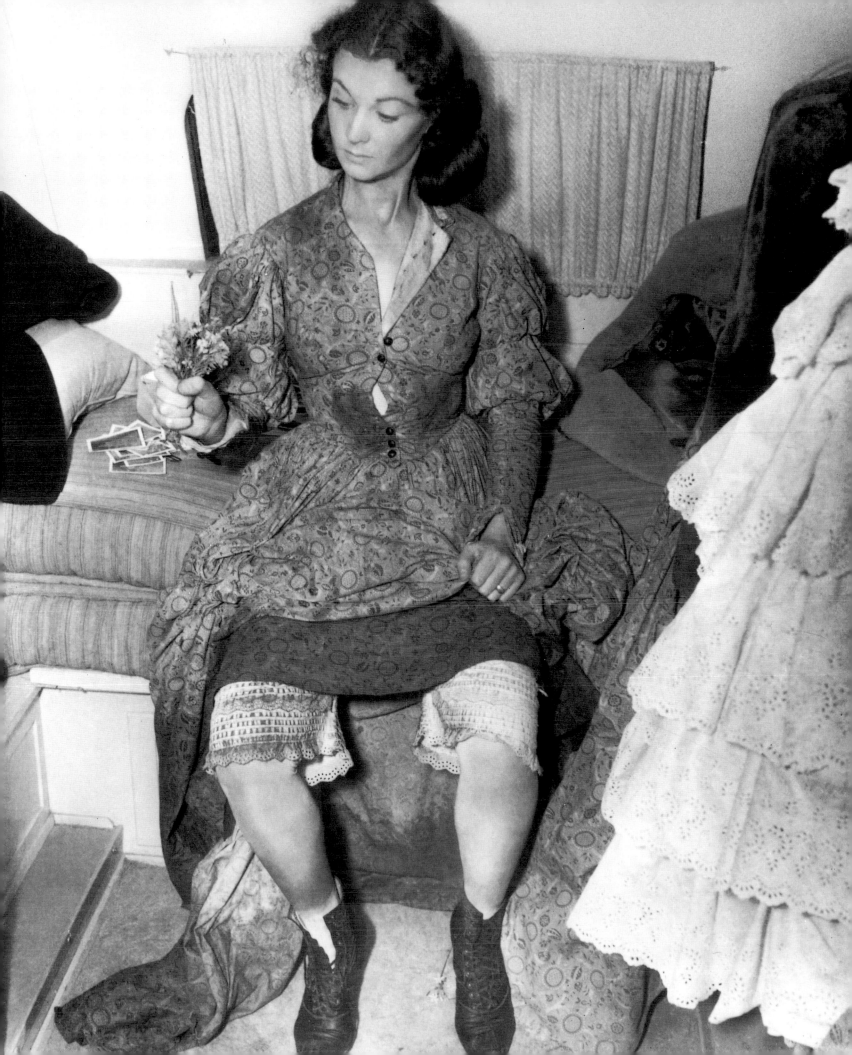

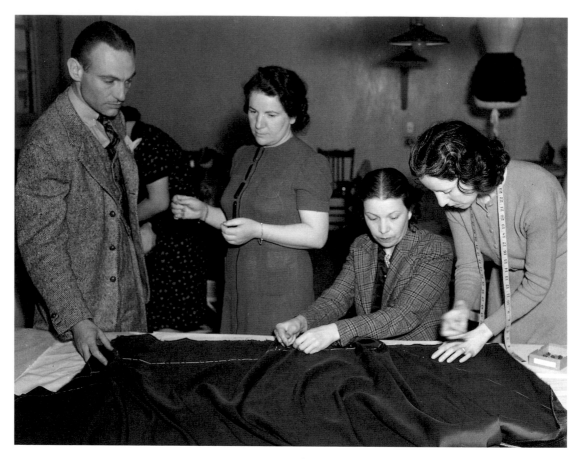

Above: Costume designer Walter Plunkett supervises the cutting of Scarlett's red dress (right). In 1935, Plunkett became so fed up with Hollywood that he quit his job at RKO and went to New York to design women's clothes. In 1936, Katharine Hepburn insisted that RKO rehire him to create the costumes for Mary of Scotland. *Back in Hollywood, Plunkett wrote Selznick a note asking for the assignment on* Gone With the Wind. *"I had done for Kate Hepburn* Little Women, *which was one of his pictures," Plunkett said in a 1981 lecture. "So he knew me and immediately — in fact, the day after my note was delivered — I got the message to come and do it."*

The actors were missing their marks and forgetting their lines. Leslie Howard had an additional problem. By June, he was also working on *Intermezzo*. Some days he moved from the set of one movie to the set of the other and then back again. But Howard, like De Havilland, was "a sweetheart to get along with," according to Kern. Howard asked the assistant directors for a little more warning when *Intermezzo* needed him. Pyschologically, he could shed Ashley and the nineteenth century in five minutes, he said, but he needed a little longer to get out of his costume.

The camera operators failed to get into position. Every scene required six, seven, ten, or thirteen takes. Even Vivien, whose accent had been impeccable, said "been" in the British fashion during Take 5 of the last scene on June 26. After ten takes of the scene, 527U, the actors were dismissed at 12:25 A.M. on June 27.

On the production log for Tuesday, June 27, there is a line of asterisks under the words "Wrapping up." Those words were hopeful but not accurate. By nightfall, Vivien Leigh and Clark Gable had finally finished. But Fleming spent the rest of the week directing small scenes with the servants at Tara and with the lesser players in Atlanta—Laura Hope Crews as Aunt Pitty, Jane Darwell as Mrs. Merriwether, Leona Roberts as Mrs. Meade, and Alicia Rhett as

Above: The famous dress made from Tara's green velvet curtains. With the help of Margaret Mitchell, Plunkett learned how clothes were made during the blockade. The women who ran the Daughters of the Confederacy museums in Savannah and Charleston gave him samples of fabric clipped from the hems of skirts and showed him how walnut seeds and stones were made into buttons and how the thorns of thorn bushes were used as pins. Facing page: Samples of plaid fabric Plunkett brought back from Atlanta were stapled to this sketch.

SCARLETT

179

Facing page: Leigh and Fleming prepare for a scene at the Twelve Oaks barbecue. Above left: An early version of the silk muslin green sprig dress Leigh is wearing in the still. Left: The green sprig dress worn in the film. Since authentic 1861 fabrics had prints too tiny to photograph well, Plunkett doubled the size of the sprigs (Collection Dennis A. Shaw and James Tumblin). Above: Scarlett not only ate well after she married Rhett, she never lacked for clothes. When he accepted his Oscar for producing Gone With the Wind, *Selznick said, "It's too bad there isn't an award for costume designing, too, because Walter Plunkett would have received it." Costume designers were not honored by the Academy until 1948. Plunkett was nominated ten times but only managed to share one Oscar, for* An American in Paris *(1951).*

Above: The dress Scarlett wore during her near rape in Shantytown (Collection Dennis A. Shaw and James Tumblin). Facing page top left: This dress was described as green in the book; Plunkett got Margaret Mitchell's permission to change the color to scarlet. Bottom left: Only the ermine jacket of this version of Scarlett's honeymoon costume was in the film. When the jacket was discovered at Western Costume Company several years ago, it was sold at auction for $16,000. The other two designs on the page were discarded (All four sketches: Collection Dennis A. Shaw and James Tumblin).

Rhett shocks staid Southern society at the Bazaar by dancing with a woman in mourning. It was the worst possible taste to wear a bonnet and veil at an evening party, and, as Susan Myrick wrote to Margaret Mitchell, "Walter Plunkett and I are plotting to get the bonnet off but we are doubtful. You see, the fools paid John Frederics of NY a hundred bucks for that bonnet and they are bound she'll wear it." (White Columns in Hollywood). *She did. Plunkett (above) designed the costumes for Selznick's* Nothing Sacred *and* Tom Sawyer *while waiting for a script on* Gone With the Wind. *Born in Oakland, California, in 1902, Plunkett graduated from the University of California at Berkeley and worked as an actor before drifting into costume design.* (Costume sketch on facing page: Collection Dennis A. Shaw and James Tumblin).

For Susan
with my very
best wishes —
Walter

Four discarded designs. Selznick was as particular about costumes as he was about sets, dialogue, and actors. Plunkett was enthusiastic about his design (bottom right) for Scarlett's dress in the New Orleans sequence, but Selznick was unwilling to spend the $1,500 it would have cost to make the costume (All four sketches: Collection Dennis A. Shaw and James Tumblin).

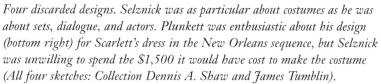

Selznick was concerned about how poorly Gable's costumes fit. "I think it is very disappointing indeed to have the elegant Rhett Butler wandering around with clothes that look as though he had bought them at the Hart, Schaffner, and Marx of that period and walked right out of the store with them."
Memo from David O. Selznick, April 3, 1939

"I made it a point to go to the bottom of the terrible mess we have made of Gable's clothes, and was surprised to find that the reason Gable looks so much worse in the clothes he has had so far in the picture . . . is that Gable was told he could have any tailor he wanted except Schmidt. Since Schmidt has been Gable's tailor all through his career, from the time he started as an obscure actor to the time he became the biggest star in the world, this was an insane order to begin with. And it had the further effect of making Gable take a what-the-hell attitude."
Memo from David O. Selznick, April 17, 1939

Holt

In this sketch by Dorothea Holt, Scarlett tries on the green bonnet Rhett has brought her from Paris. "Selznick threw out every bonnet sketch for weeks and drove Mr. John [Frederics] crazy," says Holt. Aunt Pittypat's house is considerably less cluttered here than in the movie.

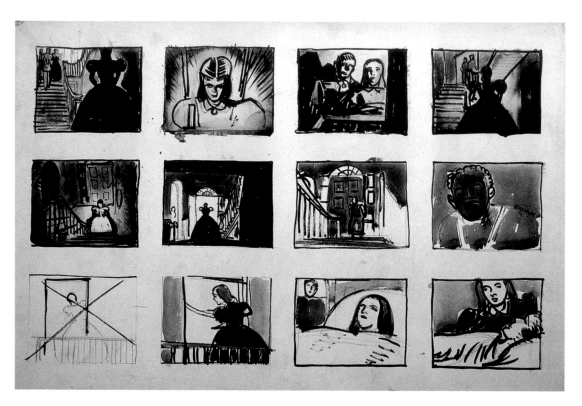

Above and above right: These story-boards which lead up to the birth of Melanie's baby during the evacuation of Atlanta are drawn in cold greenish tints, unlike Menzies's actual use of color in the film. As Menzies wrote after the film was finished, "In the birth sequence of black & yellow it helps the scene by being silhouette — more indication than fact & the yellow orange intensified the feeling of hot late afternoon." Right: Olivia de Havilland amuses herself during a costume fitting. Far right: Melanie left Atlanta in her nightgown, but she refused to leave without her brother Charles's sword, seen atop the Confederate flag in this scene rendering.

Above: Bonnie's bedroom with the floor strewn with toys. Right: The dead child is laid out in her riding costume. Cammie King, who played Bonnie, was the stepdaughter of Herbert Kalmus, the founder of Technicolor. Cammie's older sister was originally cast as Bonnie but outgrew the part when the production was delayed.

Ashley's sister India. Alicia Rhett was the only actress who had been cast through Cukor's long search for Scarlett in the South, although a few of the actors, including Evelyn Keyes, had originally come from Atlanta.

When the filming was over, according to Ridgeway Callow, Olivia De Havilland and Leslie Howard graciously thanked the crew members. Gable and Fleming "walked right off the set without saying good-by."

Despite everything, the look of the movie had remained steady. On January 28, two days after shooting started, Selznick had repeated his command that Menzies was to be in sole control of the color. Selznick informed his director, his cinematographer, and, most of all, the intrusive representatives of Technicolor who demanded bright, harsh lighting, that "It is up to Mr. Menzies to decide whether a pattern or color is going to be too obtrusive or is dangerous from any standpoint. . . . He has the privilege of making a test of any material or color any time he sees fit. . . . Where he feels reasonably safe, his decisions should be made without tests—but in any event, his decisions should be final." That was one area in which Selznick never wavered. He was determined that, no matter how much it cost him, *Gone With the Wind* would be, visually, the most breathtaking movie ever made.

Selznick's extraordinary attention to detail can be seen in these two "Jack Jumped over the Candlestick" drawings. Although the wallpaper in Bonnie's bedroom was barely visible in the movie, there are dozens of such detailed renderings.

195

"Grotesque shadows play on the gaily decorated walls of the nursery."
Gone With the Wind *screenplay*

Above: After each scene, the actors would stay in position, while a camera operator moved in front of the camera holding a three-sided white card called a Lilly. Then another three or four feet of film were run. The Lilly allowed the laboratory to check whether the cameramen were shooting with the proper front light and key lights. When color film became easier to use and less expensive to process, the Lilly was no longer necessary. Facing page: A camera lens box belonging to Arthur Arling, the principal camera operator on Gone With the Wind *(Collection Dennis A. Shaw and James Tumblin).*

Menzies was gone by the second week in July. Selznick had loaned him to Alexander Korda to design the remake of *The Thief of Bagdad*. In 1924, the young art director had convinced Douglas Fairbanks to let him design the original *Thief of Bagdad*, and the brilliance of Menzies's work had made his reputation. Menzies sailed for England on July 12. During the summer and fall, it was Selznick who safeguarded the look of the movie as he put the reels together with film editors Hal Kern and Jim Newcom.

August and September were Jack Cosgrove's months, the making of magic by trickery, including blending thousands of feet of real skies with the false skies that would make the real more beautiful. The infinite detail required of Cosgrove's matte department included making sure that the painted trees, foliage, and plowed fields were accurate for dozens of scenes that occurred in every season over more than a decade. For one scene, Cosgrove was required to add both the cow Scarlett brought back to Tara and the cow's reflection in the water.

Victor Fleming and the actors came back in October: Butterfly McQueen for two days of retakes at $33.34 a day, Evelyn Keyes for one day at $250 a week, Fleming for two weeks at $4,000 a week, Vivien Leigh and Olivia de Havilland at $208.33 a day. The last scene Vivien shot—on Saturday, October 14—was the same one which had been shot on the first day of production nine months earlier, Scarlett flirting with the Tarleton boys on the porch of Tara.

Facing page, above: Mervyn LeRoy (seated) has driven the mile from M-G-M to Selznick's studio to discuss The Wizard of Oz, *which LeRoy produced and Fleming directed and then abandoned when Selznick and L. B. Mayer asked him to take on* Gone With the Wind (The Fred A. Parrish Collection). *(King Vidor replaced Fleming on* The Wizard of Oz, *but received no credit.) Facing page, below: Plunkett shows Fleming sketches for Melanie's costumes while Olivia de Havilland looks on. Left: Sam Wood (seated) was* Gone With the Wind's *third director. Looking over Wood's shoulder is the movie's second cinematographer, Ernest Haller. Below: Technicolor cameraman Ray Rennahan (left) takes a light reading (The Fred A. Parrish Collection).*

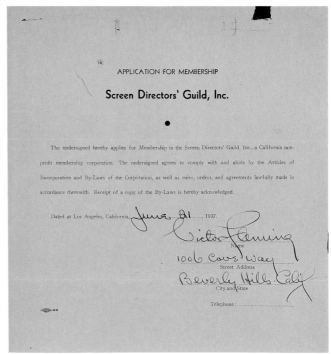

Facing page, above: Fleming directs the girls during their nap after the Twelve Oaks barbecue. Evelyn Keyes is face up in the right foreground, while Menzies stands near the foot of the bed. Susan Myrick, standing with arms crossed, was Margaret Mitchell's friend and the movie's arbiter of southern taste (The Fred A. Parrish Collection). Facing page, below: Fleming's application for membership in the Screen Directors Guild is dated June 1937. The guild had been formed a year earlier, but it was not recognized by the studios until 1939 (Collection Dennis A. Shaw and James Tumblin). Above: Selznick paid Warner Bros. $600 a week for Ernest Haller, who was one of Bette Davis's favorite cinematographers and who had made her remarkably beautiful in Jezebel. *Haller probably earned less than $600, since studios charged a premium when they lent other studios their actors and technicians.*

The technicians prepare for one of Gone With the Wind's *spectacular crane shots. Ray Rennahan, the cameraman rented to Selznick by Technicolor, is seated left on the camera platform; the man on the right is Arthur Arling, who was the principal camera operator. Arling's assistant, Harry Wolf, is standing left of the crane and holding Arling's lens box (Collection Dennis A. Shaw and James Tumblin). Facing page:* Gone With the Wind's *souvenir program originally exaggerated the number of extras used in the movie. Selznick, who felt no exaggeration was necessary, wrote the following sentence: "In addition to the 59 members of the cast, there were over 12,000 days of employment given to over 2,400 extra and bit people."*

The biggest winner on *Gone With the Wind* was the man who had taken the biggest gamble. But David Selznick, too uncontrolled and undisciplined a gambler ever to leave the Clover Club with any chips, was also the biggest loser. It was Vivien Leigh for whom the triumph was unmixed. She would win an Oscar and Olivier. And, if that marriage would end twenty years later during her terrible slide into manic-depression, well, life, unlike movies, is not a land of happy endings.

Selznick tried to get Victor Fleming to allow him to give Sam Wood and Bill Menzies credit as associate directors, but Fleming was enraged at the idea. Yet *Gone With the Wind* brought Wood something more important than a screen credit—a lasting relationship with Menzies. Wood was not a brilliant director, but he was smart enough to turn his movies over to Menzies, to the benefit of *King's Row* and *For Whom the Bell Tolls*, in particular. Wood directed the actors, the area where Menzies was weakest; Menzies created the look of the films. On *For Whom the Bell Tolls*, said Technicolor cameraman Ray Rennahan, "Sam leaned on him one hundred percent. Bill designed the costumes, the locations, the compositions."

There were other winners. Hattie McDaniel was the first black nominated by the Academy and the first black winner of an Academy Award; in a speech prepared by the studio, she pledged to be a credit to her race. Hal Kern, Jim Newcom, Ernest Haller (who had replaced Lee Garmes as cinematographer), Ray Rennahan, Lyle Wheeler, and Menzies also won Academy Awards.

Olivia de Havilland lost as supporting actress to McDaniel, but *Gone With the Wind* elevated her to an importance she would not otherwise have had. Within a decade De Havilland would win two Oscars for best actress—in 1946 for *To Each His Own* and in 1949 for *The Heiress*. Yet

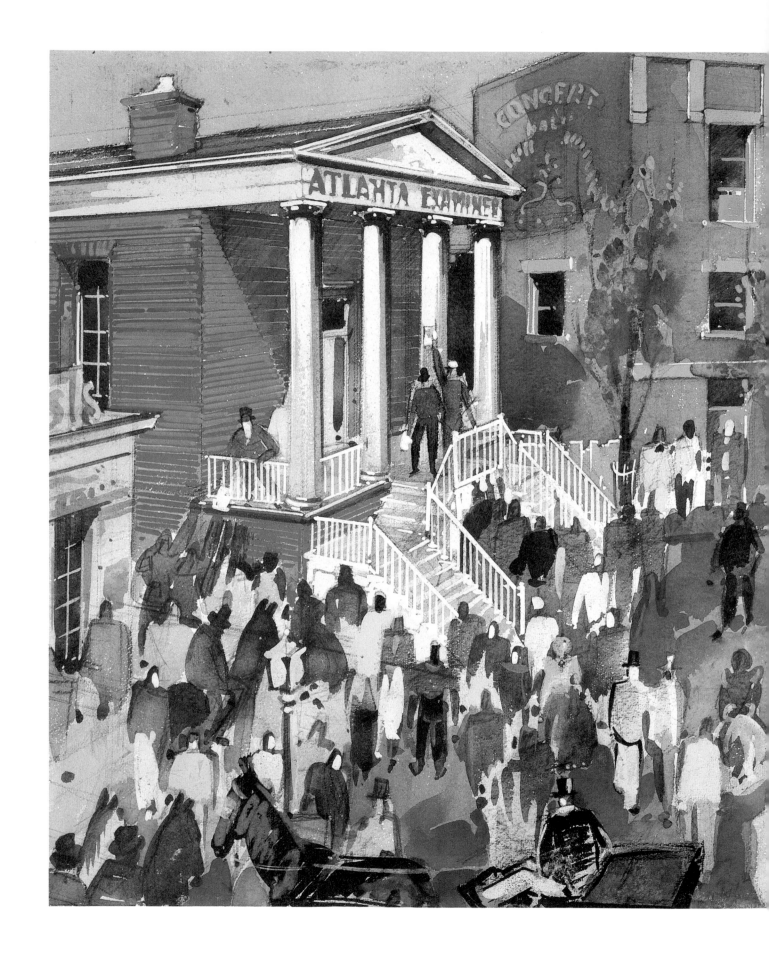

Jack Cosgrove added the engine
smoke to this scene of citizens
in front of the Atlanta Examiner
building.

she is remembered less for those movies than for *Gone With the Wind*. And, a bit like Melanie whose sweetness covered steel, Olivia would do what defiant Bette Davis had been unable to do: weaken the studio contract system. When her seven-year contract with Warner Bros. ended in 1943, she won a court case that kept the studios from adding to their contracts the months or years a player had been on suspension. A seven-year contract meant a maximum of seven years, said the courts. Anything more was peonage.

Jock Whitney won no awards for his participation in *Gone With the Wind*, but when he moved on after dabbling in movies for eight years, he had earned $1.5 million on a $2 million investment. He lived a golden life. When as an Air Force colonel in World War II, he was captured by the Germans, he escaped within three weeks. His Greentree Stables was filled with winning horses. President Eisenhower appointed him Ambassador to England, and, for a while, he published the *New York Herald Tribune*. A hundred million dollars helps, of course, and Jock's days were sunny until almost the end, in February 1982.

Olivia de Havilland still survives, as do the actor and actresses who played her brother Charles and Scarlett's younger sisters. And Brent Tarleton (Fred Crane) has recently made a second career of sailing on cruise ships lecturing about *Gone With the Wind*.

Leslie Howard returned to England and produced, directed, and starred in patriotic films during the early years of the war. In 1943, in a scene that could have come from one of those films, his airplane was shot down as he flew from Lisbon to London. There was a rumor that his plane was a decoy because Prime Minister Winston Churchhill was flying that day. It is also possible that his death was merely an accident of war.

All the important members of the crew are also gone, and Margaret Mitchell was killed by a taxi in 1949 as she crossed Peachtree Street, where so many scenes in her novel took place.

David Selznick died in 1965. Irene had left him in 1945 when he was already deep in an affair with Jennifer Jones, whom he married four years later. He starred Jennifer in a series of movies from *Duel in the Sun* (1946) and *Portrait of Jennie* (1948) to *A Farewell to Arms* (1957) and, in his last years, did little but stage manage her career. Irene had not left him because of Jennifer. She had simply turned to him in bed one night and said, "The jig's up." Living with David had finally become too much. "I didn't want more out of life," she wrote in her autobiography. "I wanted less. Less of excess."

David had wanted to create the greatest movie ever made. For most moviegoers in 1939—and for more than a few in 1996—he had succeeded. But that success came at the cost of his studio and, in the end, of his self confidence. How can you top yourself after you've made *Gone With the Wind*? Selling his stake in *Gone With the Wind* made David solvent. If he had lived or worked with even a touch of financial caution, he wouldn't have been $9.5 million in debt to banks six years later. But if he hadn't lived extravagantly and spent unnecessary millions on his movies, he wouldn't have been David O. Selznick. The causes of David's success and of his failure were the same. To his benefit and his peril, he was obsessive, indecisive, recklessly extravagant, undisciplined, and too much of a perfectionist to settle for less than what he considered the best. Whatever his faults, David dreamed big.

Long before 1965, the movies had changed on him. Television had replaced films as America's mass entertainment, and the government had crippled the movie industry by forcing a divorce between the studios and the theater chains that owned them. In 1951, walking with Ben Hecht through a deserted Hollywood at dawn, David called Hollywood a new Egypt: "Full

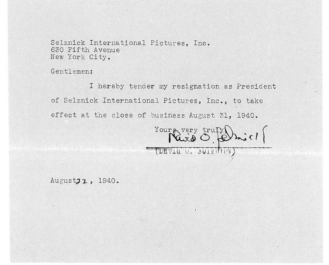

Selznick International Pictures, Inc.
630 Fifth Avenue
New York City.

Gentlemen:

I hereby tender my resignation as President
of Selznick International Pictures, Inc., to take
effect at the close of business August 31, 1940.

Yours very truly,

(DAVID O. SELZNICK)

August 22, 1940.

Left: David Selznick in his studio office where he "lived" up to twenty-four hours a day during the making of Gone With the Wind *(Courtesy Daniel Mayer Selznick). Above: Less than nine months after* Gone With the Wind's *triumphant debut and less than five months after the movie swept the Academy Awards, David O. Selznick resigned as president of Selznick International Pictures (Collection Dennis A. Shaw and James Tumblin). In 1941, the studio was liquidated.*

of crumbling pyramids" that would keep on crumbling "until finally the wind blows the last studio prop across the sands."

David wrote poetry—sentimental doggerel—all his life. As a writer, his gift was for rewriting, and his comment rewrites Percy Bysshe Shelley's "Ozymandias." It would not be accurate to say that David O. Selznick's life echoed Shelley's forgotten king whose broken statue is merely a colossal wreck among the lone and level and boundless sands. Movies have a way of sticking around—at least those movies that can stand the test of time. The pyramids may crumble. *"Gone With the Wind"* remains.

Preview

★

Gone With the Wind

(Drama)

In some ways the most herculean film task ever undertaken, 'Gone With the Wind' appears finally as one of the screen's major achievements, meriting highest respect and plaudits, and poised for grosses which may be second to none in the history of the business.

It may be conceded that every theatre-goer, every reader of Margaret Mitchell's enormously successful book, plus many who may not have read it and many who go seldom to shows, will want to view this superlative picturization. Every customer, by word of mouth, will serve to swell this insured patronage.

The result amply justifies the vast patience, the confidence, the showman's faith and courage, the time consumed and even the soaring expense which David O. Selznick put behind his production labors to do the thing with perfection and pride of craft.

The most important invitation the exhibitor may give his clientele is the assurance that the picture is an exact visual reproduction of the book. What telescoping of the voluminous text was essential to bring it within even the long playing time of three hours and 40 minutes represents a remarkable screen writing triumph and directorial achievement. Familiars of the Mitchell narrative see no discrepancies, no noticeable deletions. It is all there, in its full dramatic force. The identity of the players will be hailed as the characters come to vital and tragic life, flesh-and-blood creatures every one, from the stellar group to the least of the bit performers.

Under the inspirational mood which executive guidance and professional challenge managed to create, despite the obstacles and production agonies encountered, every role is etched unforgettably through the trials, the passions, the antagonisms, the bitterness and sweetness which goad the characters to their deeds of valor or petty selfishness against the grandiose sweep of the Civil War and what followed it in the final phase of a chivalry which vanished with the wind.

Clark Gable, as was anticipated, is Rhett Butler to the life. He plays it with simple, direct frankness; the hard surface of the cynical, almost barbaric man of experience, and the heartbreak of the husband and father after he has married Scarlett, trying desperately to hide his emotions—all with heroic proportion; the man who found more heart in the harlot Belle Watling than his frantic, unpredictable wife. It is a great job.

Vivien Leigh, as one watches, fascinated, her perfect artistry and emotional facility in creating the girl-woman, Scarlett O'Hara, builds and leaves the impression that no other feminine star could have done so completely satisfactory an enactment of this passionate and cynical opportunist. The tragic phases of the character, from the first flirtatious assurance through the successive escapades and marriages, which never quite abated her true love for Ashley Wilkes, are all flawlessly expressed. She steeps the role in a great, haunting sadness of memorable quality.

Leslie Howard perfectly comprehends the gentle, dreamy, deliberately loyal but sorely tempted Ashley,loving his wife, Melanie, and beloved by her and their mutual friend, Scarlett.

Equal to any of her co-stars in merited applause for a superb piece of artistry as Melanie, the gentle, loyal, completely unselfish aristocrat, is Olivia de Havilland, lifting herself to a new level of first importance.

Another truly great performance is Hattie McDaniel's mammy role, the outspoken old retainer whose wild grief at the tragic break between Rhett and Scarlett when their young daughter dies is a masterpiece of provocative emotion.

Thomas Mitchell admirably delivers the likeness of the wild and lovable Gerald O'Hara, sire of Scarlett and her volatile temperament. Sharply imprinted from amongst the numerous supporting cast are the portrayals of Barbara O'Neil as Ellen O'Hara, Laura Hope Crews, the fluttery and fainting Aunt Pittypat; Harry Davenport as Doctor Meade, Evelyn Keyes and Ann Rutherford, respectively the younger sisters of Scarlett, Suellen and Carreen; Alicia Rhett as India, Ona Munson in a splendid and sympathetically projected Belle Watling, the Atlanta brothel madame; Carroll Nye, the unhappy second husband of Scarlett, and Rand Brooks as her first boyish spouse.

Deserving special mention for a remarkable performance as the childlike, terrified and pitiable negro maid, Prissy, is Butterfly McQueen, whose part takes on much importance. Zack Williams and Everett Brown also are standouts as the loyal household and field slaves. Victor Jory scores in the carpetbagger part, and with him in brief but excellent showing, Isabel Jewell.

Honorable mention furthermore must go also to Howard Hickman, Marcella Martin, Leona Roberts, Jane Darwell, Mary Anderson, Eddie Anderson (Rochester) in a brief role, Cliff Edwards, George Hackathorne, Roscoe Ates, John Arledge, Eric Linden, Tom Tyler, Paul Hurst, George Meeker and Wallis Clark, Irving Bacon, Ward Bond, Cammie King as the child Bonnie Blue Butler, Mickey Kuhn, Lillian Kemble Cooper and a number of others of high talent with whom the cast is studded.

Victor Fleming's direction is a mainstay of the picture's superlative quality as an artistic triumph and top entertainment value. His was a gigantic task, physically as well as mentally. He progressed the story masterfully. The characters are kept clean-cut. The episodes are dramatically rounded out and punctuated, the individual scenes crisp, appropriately timed, the infinite shadings neatly accomplished, the dramatic highlights socked with almost oppressive emotional power. Intimacies and sweeps, love scenes and battle, minor tragedies marching into the great national drama of a lost cause besieged by the inevitable hour of change—all are faultlessly managed by Fleming.

The screen play by Sidney Howard comes as close to exemplary perfection as the screen may approximate in spirit and letter to the book

Continued on page 6

Preview Credits

David O. Selznick production for Metro release.

Stars and their roles:

RHETT BUTLER . . . . CLARK GABLE
ASHLEY WILKES . . LESLIE HOWARD
MELANIE HAMILTON OLIVIA de HAVILLAND
SCARLETT O'HARA . . . VIVIEN LEIGH

Supporting players and their parts:

BRENT TARLETON . . . GEORGE REEVES
STUART TARLETON . . . FRED CRANE
MAMMY . . . . HATTIE McDANIEL
BIG SAM . . . . EVERETT BROWN
ELIJAH . . . . . . ZACK WILLIAMS
GERALD O'HARA . . THOMAS MITCHELL
PORK . . . . OSCAR POLK
ELLEN O'HARA . . . BARBARA O'NEIL
JONAS WILKERSON . . . . VICTOR JORY
SUELLEN O'HARA . . . EVELYN KEYES
CARREEN O'HARA . ANN RUTHERFORD
PRISSY . . . . . BUTTERFLY McQUEEN
JOHN WILKES . . . . HOWARD HICKMAN
INDIA WILKES . . . . . ALICIA RHETT
CHARLES HAMILTON . . RAND BROOKS
FRANK KENNEDY . . . . CARROLL NYE
CATHLEEN CALVERT MARCELLA MARTIN
AUNT "PITTYPAT" HAMILTON LAURA HOPE CREWS
DOCTOR MEADE . . HARRY DAVENPORT
MRS. MEADE . . . LEONA ROBERTS
MRS. MERRIWETHER . JANE DARWELL
RENE PICARD . . . . ALBERT MORIN
MAYBELLE MERRIWETHER MARY ANDERSON
FANNY ELSING . . . . TERRY SHERO
OLD LEVI . . . . WILLIAM McCLAIN
UNCLE PETER . . . EDDIE ANDERSON
PHIL MEADE . . . . . JACKIE MORAN
REMINISCENT SOLDIER, CLIFF EDWARDS
BELLE WATLING . . . . ONA MUNSON
THE SERGEANT . . . . . ED CHANDLER
A WOUNDED SOLDIER IN PAIN GEORGE HACKATHORNE
A CONVALESCENT SOLDIER ROSCOE ATES
A DYING SOLDIER . . JOHN ARLEDGE
AN AMPUTATION CASE . ERIC LINDEN
A COMMANDING OFFICER . TOM TYLER
A MOUNTED OFFICER WILLIAM BAKEWELL
THE BARTENDER . . . . LEE PHELPS
A YANKEE DESERTER . . . PAUL HURST
THE CARPETBAGGER'S FRIEND ERNEST WHITMAN
A RETURNING VETERAN WILLIAM STELLING
A HUNGRY SOLDIER, LOUIS JEAN HEYDT
EMMY SLATTERY . . . ISABEL JEWELL
THE YANKEE MAJOR . ROBERT ELLIOTT
HIS POKER-PLAYING CAPTAINS GEORGE MEEKER, WALLIS CLARK
THE CORPORAL . . . . IRVING BACON
A CARPETBAGGER ORATOR ADRIAN MORRIS
JOHNNY GALLEGHER . J. M. KERRIGAN
A YANKEE BUSINESSMAN OLIN HOWLAND
A RENEGADE . . . . YAKIMA CANUTT
HIS COMPANION . BLUE WASHINGTON
TOM, A YANKEE CAPTAIN, WARD BOND
BONNIE BLUE BUTLER . CAMMIE KING
BEAU WILKES . . . . . MICKEY KUHN
BONNIE'S NURSE LILLIAN KEMBLE COOPER

Directed by Victor Fleming.

Produced by David O. Selznick.

Screen play by Sidney Howard, based on Margaret Mitchell's novel of old South.

Production designed by William Cameron Menzies. Art direction by Lyle Wheeler. Photographed by Ernest Haller. Technicolor associates, Ray Rennahan, Wilfrid M. Cline. Musical score by Max Steiner. Associate, Lou Forbes. Special photographic effects by Jack Cosgrove, Associate (fire effects), Lee Zavitz. Costumes designed by Walter Plunkett. Scarlett's hats by John Frederics. Interiors by Joseph B. Platt. Interior decoration by Edward G. Boyle. Supervising film editor, Hal C. Kern. Associate film editor, James E. Newcom. Scenario assistant, Barbara Keon. Recorder, Frank Maher. Makeup and hair styling, Monty Westmore. Associates, Hazel Rogers, Ben Nye. Dance directors, Frank Floyd, Eddie Prinz. Historian, Wilbur G. Kurtz. Technical advisers, Susan Myrick, Will Price. Research, Lillian K. Deighton. Production manager, Raymond A. Klune. Technicolor Co. supervisor, Natalie Kalmus. Associate, Henri Jaffa. Assistant director, Eric G. Stacey. Second assistant director, Ridgeway Callow. In charge of wardrobe, Edward P. Lambert. Casting managers, Charles Richards, Fred Schuessler. Assistant film editors, Richard Van Enger, Ernest Leadley.

Previewed at Four Star theatre, Dec. 12. Running time 3 hours and 40 mins.

'Gone' Offers Rich Possibilities For Exploitation—

'Gone With the Wind' is a natural from the standpoint of publicity and exploitation. Exhibitors will find a wealth of selling material which should return rich box office harvests. Not in years has a screen feature presented such a diversion of selling angles.

With the millions of readers of the book, it can safely be estimated there's a possible waiting audience of 50,000,000 to 65,000,000 awaiting the advent of the screen version.

The tremendous sale of the Margaret Mitchell novel is an angle no exhibitor would overlook. That, alone, will probably be responsible for more ticket sales than any other angle. Then, too, stress can be laid in all advertising and publicity on the time element that had elapsed between the buying of the yarn by David O. Selznick and the finished screen version, something quite unique in the industry.

Advertising matter, both advance and current, should be entirely of the dignified type, to give the screen version the dollar and a half flavor it richly merits. Particularly should this be true of the two-a-day road show engagements which will take precedence for at least the next 12 months.

RICH WITH NAMES

From the standpoint of names, 'Gone With the Wind' is rich in exploitation values. Topping these names is Clark Gable who makes a living counterpart of the Rhett Butler character. Too much stress cannot be laid on the Gable performance. Likewise, exhibs can go to town in spreading the name of Vivien Leigh all over their marquees and in every bit of advertising and publicity. Miss Leigh comes through with a performance of Scarlett O'Hara that would have delighted the author before she penned the thousand odd pages making up the yarn.

By way of additional cast names there are Leslie Howard, Olivia de Havilland, Thomas Mitchell, Hattie McDaniel, Ona Munson, Laura Hope Crews, Cliff Edwards, George Hackathorne, Roscoe Ates, Eric Linden, Isabel Jewell, Eddie (Rochester) Anderson, Paul Hurst—all names that mean something at the box office. Exhibs can cash in on these marquee decorations.

WORD OF MOUTH BALLY

Word-of-mouth advertising will be one of the important factors in selling 'Gone' to theatre audiences, both in the two-a-day runs and in the subsequents when picture finally is generally released. Despite its overlength, bulk of patrons will regret the final fadeout.

Innumerable tieup opportunities are afforded wide-awake showmen, who can take advantage of the color stills to secure widespread window representation. The picture, it must be noted, is entirely in Technicolor and exhibs will not fail to acquaint their clientele with this fact. Some of the color sequences are pictorially perfect and art students will rave over the soft hues and dazzling color schemes with which the picture is dotted.

Theatre operators in the South, especially, will be interested in the depicting of the reconstruction days

♣ Continued on page 6 ♣

Daily Variety, *December 13, 1939 (Courtesy of the Academy of Motion Picture Arts and Sciences).*

Directors Win Six Of 15 Spots On Acad Board—

Directors captured six of 15 posts on new board of directors of Academy of Motion Picture Arts & Sciences. Two, however, Frank Capra and Mervin LeRoy, carry classification of producer-director. Three actors were elected, three producers, two writers and one technician.

New board will consist of Frank Capra, who has declared himself for re-election as prexy; Ronald Colman, C. B. DeMille, Howard Estabrook, Clark Gable, Mervin LeRoy, Frank Lloyd, Robert Riskin, David O. Selznick, Douglas Shearer, James Stewart, Norman Taurog, Walter Wanger, Sam Wood, Darryl F. Zanuck.

First meeting of new board is scheduled for Tuesday (19) when new officers will be elected. Rules do not require that officers must be elected from among board members. Walt Disney is already being mentioned for prexy, with others favoring selection of Sam Wood or Frank Lloyd.

Annual awards committee also will meet Tuesday to complete plans for banquet tentatively scheduled for Feb. 29.

Stoll Elected Prexy Of Western Electric—

New York, Dec. 12.—Clarence G. Stoll was elected president of Western Electric Co. at meeting of board of directors today, and succeeds Edgar S. Bloom on latter's retirement Dec. (31). Stoll, 36 years with the company, has been vice-president in charge of operations since 1928. Bloom, retiring at 65 in line with Bell system regulations, ends 43 years of service and will become director of purchases for the British Purchasing Commission.

WB 'Virginia City' Troupe Pulls Out—

Warners 'Virginia City' troupe pulled out for Victorville late yesterday following series of deferred starts due to casting and weather conditions. Unit, which includes 122 persons, will spend three days on Mojave river location. Errol Flynn, Miriam Hopkins, Randolph Scott, Humphrey Bogart, Alan Hale, Frank McHugh, Douglas Dumbrille, Guinn Williams and John Litel are making trip.

20th on Title Hunt

20th-Fox currently is seeking titles for four features skedded to go into work within next two weeks. First on list is 'Twinkle, Twinkle Little Star,' based on biography of Linda Darnell, who has title role. Others are 'Sweetheart of Turret One,' 'Cisco Kid', No. 2, and 'Hotel For Women', No. 2.

Briefie on Pic Dogs

Del Frazier on Monday turns cameras on canines belonging to Errol Flynn, Bette Davis and other Warners stars for briefie titled 'Famous Movie Dogs.' Picture will be shot on Burbank lot.

Reeves on 'Doctors'

Theodore Reeves has completed treatment and will do screenplay for Republic's 'Doctors Don't Tell,' John H. Auer producing.

Film Preview

◄ Continued from page 3 ◄

he translated and its inner essence. It has stature and dignity, excitement, marked historic significance, excellent selectivity and complete authenticity in character and treatment. Dialog is of the finest; the narrative titles memorable. Griefs, loves, passions, strange and natural, noble and despicable behavior are given a tremendous human and dramatic blending in heroic proportion.

The siege of Atlanta and its burning and the hammering march of Sherman to the sea is terrific in spectacle and agonizing realism — and desolating the scenes in the Atlanta improvised hospital with the innumerable wounded. These scenes and others are not pretty, not picturesquely dramatic—they are fierce and ugly and tragically disturbing as they had to be to visualize the book.

But beautiful, gorgeous is the Technicolor which invests the whole with prismatic glory. Brilliantly painted with the newest processes of the medium. And far beyond the ordinary quality is the camera work

of Ernest Haller and the Technicolor associates, Ray Rennahan and Wilfred M. Cline. Exceptional too, the production design by William Cameron Menzies; the art direction of Lyle Wheeler; the photographic effects by Jack Cosgrove and Lee Zavits (fire effects); the haunting emphasis placed upon the drama by the fine musical score of Max Steiner and his associate, Lou Forbes.

Costumes designed by Walter Plunkett rate highest praise, and the interiors by Joseph B. Platt, the decorations by Edward G. Boyle, the appropriate properties to give the authentic southern atmosphere of the time, under management of Harold Coles.

The treatment of the picture will not offend the South. It is designed and achieved to eliminate any Dixie resentment; lauds the valor of its soldiery; lays some brunt upon the Yankee; in no way offends the pride of the traditional Old South, now an echo in the winds, and its inheritors and theatre patrons . . . A great picture, by every measure.

Retakes
BY GEORGE E. PHAIR

▼ Continued from page 2 ▼

of London in Ashley's accent, which was not unnatural. Gentlemen of the Old South often studied in England, when they had the dough.

★ ★ ★

A resume of the game reveals that the boys and gals played safe in the first half—sort of feeling each other out. In the second half they cut loose with everything in the dramatic program, Scarlett running with the ball, Melanie blocking, Butler intercepting passes and Ashley calling for time out after every play because he bruised so easily, and besides, he was too honorable to slug.

★ ★ ★

In rain and shine and love and war
The epic marches on.
At least it rates an Oscar for
The Marathon.

David Rose Due in Sat. for Par Sesh—

David Rose is slated to train in Saturday for Paramount studio conferences here. Rose, who is Paramount's executive producer in England, will also view 'French Without Tears,' his final picture before abandonment of production because of war.

Vaude in Nebraska

Lincoln, Neb., Dec. 12.—'French Folies,' Sollie Child's vaude-unit, ran up $2,300 on first three days here at the Liberty. Was first flesh show in 26 months.

Polishing Mountain

Lew Foster is putting the final polish this week on the Paramount script 'Comin' 'Round the Mountain,' which William C. Thomas will produce.

Ill in Pix

EDDIE COLLINS, 20th-Fox comic, leaves St. Luke's hospital, Pasadena, Sunday for home to complete recuperation from recent appendectomy.

EDGAR BERGEN is convalescing at home following siege at St. Vincent's hospital with an infected cheek.

HENRY SCHUSTER, Par electrician, discharged from Santa Monica hospital after operation.

FRANK LOESSER at Cedars of Lebanon hospital, a flu victim.

Irene Dunne Slated For Col Doctor Pic—

Columbia is planning a production based on the life of Elizabeth Blackwell, first woman doctor, who entered practice in 1849. Irene Dunne is slated for the lead. Everett Riskin is at the production helm and is endeavoring to set Lloyd C. Douglas to plot story.

'Lone Wolf' Editing

Columbia's second of this season's 'Lone Wolf' series went to the editing lab yesterday. Pic is titled 'The Lone Wolf Strikes' and toplines Warren William and Joan Perry.

Brennan on 'Turret'

Frederick Hazlitt Brennan goes to 20th-Fox to screen play 'Sweetheart of Turret One,' Frank Wead story. H. N. Swanson agented.

Bainter Krafting

Fay Bainter set for guest shot on the Kraft Music Hall ether show through Sam Jaffe office.

Smith on 'Florian'

Leonard Smith has been added to battery of cameramen on Metro's 'Florian.'

'Gone' Offers Rich Possibilities For Exploitation—

♣ Continued from page 3 ♣

from which a great empire has been carved.

Love interest, of varying degrees, runs throughout the picture, and the unselfish love of Miss de Havilland, as Melanie, contrasted with the selfish love of Scarlett can be made the subject of essay contests in which participants may be ranged from high school youngsters to women of all other ages. Love for home, or tradition, also may be worked up to a high degree, and also the patriotic love of a people for their cherished traditions.

GOLDEN HARVEST

For those seeking to inject a little of the comedy interest, picture affords several sequences on which exhibs can cash in. To enumerate all of the selling possibilities of the picture is impossible here. That it is a natural for audience selling must be repeated.

Approached with a showmanship viewpoint, with advantage taken of the many angles afforded, 'Gone With the Wind' can have only one answer at the box office—a harvest of golden response.

Vice-Prez Run-off For Boothmen—

Run-off election will be staged Dec. 26 for office of vice-president of Moving Picture Operators, Local 150, International Alliance of Theatrical Stage Employes, between J. B. Kenton, incumbent, and R. L. MacDonald. Kenton polled 125 votes at Monday's primary against 118 registered for MacDonald. John Maynard, third candidate, received 66 votes and was eliminated.

R. L. Haywood was re-elected business representative over G. J. Schaffer and incumbent executive board, comprising W. H. Fife, R. L. Haskell, E. L. Robbins, W. G. Crowley and L. D. Mitchell was re-elected.

Other officers were filled by acclamation.

Morros Stays East On 'People' Setup—

New York, Dec. 12.—Boris Morros is remaining here for another week to carry on negotiations for screen rights to 'We The People' radio program, which he wants to make for RKO release. Deal is near closing.

15 Acts for Masquers

Masquers Club has lined up 15 acts for its 'Night At the Palace' dinner and show Friday night. William Davidson will preside at affair with Joe Ratliff as emcee. Among those set for bill are Joe Frisco, Harry Lash, Johnny Boyle, Hubert Brill, Caites Brothers, Jim O'Brien, Pat Moran, Gene Clark, Syd Saylor, Spencer Chaters, Harry Bradley, Max Waizman and Emil Seidel.

Barnes Gets Chore

George Barnes has been assigned camera chore on 20th-Fox sequel to 'Hotel For Women.'

'GONE WITH THE WIND' MAGNIFICENT; SUPREME TRIUMPH OF FILM HISTORY

Vivien Leigh Matchless Scarlett; Shares Top Honors With Clark Gable In David Selznick's Crowning Effort

In attempting to convey on paper some adequate conception of what David O. Selznick's production of "Gone With the Wind" actually is like, one is confronted with the discouraging fact that there are no words which can truly portray something which is at one and the same time an overwhelming emotional experience, the peak milestone in motion picture achievement, an unforgettable picturization of a gracious way of living—the most gracious America ever has known—which is gone and the desolating tragedy of its violent passing, and the living incarnation of a group of human beings who have become the intimates of millions through the pages of Margaret Mitchell's book.

This is more than the greatest motion picture which ever was made. It is the ultimate realization of the dreams of what might be done in every phase of film wizardry, in production, performance, screen writing, photography, and every other of the multitude of technical operations which enter into the making of a picture.

It has everything; drama of such intensity that it tears one to shreds, laughter where laughter is fitting, horror that is meaningful, spectacle unsurpassed in screen history, characterization which will become immortal in screen annals and, above all, a breath-taking loveliness which holds one spellbound from the first dazzling blaze of color to the final fadeout. For three hours and 45 minutes, its magic unfolds on the screen, yet the end seems to come too soon.

Impact Is Terrific

From every conceivable angle, the impact of the picture upon one's senses and emotions is terrific and it never lets one down. The intermission which divides the picture is a sheer physical necessity. The tremendous sweep and dynamic power of the first half of the picture, climaxed in the staggering, awe-inspiring capture and destruction of Atlanta is so overwhelming as to leave one limp. It bespeaks the technical perfection of the picture's construction that the second half begins on a quieter yet no less powerful tone which permits the audience to recover itself in a measure and prepare for the searing personal drama which follows.

David Selznick has kept his promise to the world. He has given us Margaret Mitchell's story just as it was written. He has not changed a scene nor a character. In so doing, he has demonstrated what motion pictures can do with great stories given the respect which is their authors' due. For this is Margaret Mitchell's story immeasurably more vivid and real than it ever could hope to be on the printed page. Here are Scarlett O'Hara, Rhett Butler, Ashley Wilkes, Melanie Hamilton, Gerald O'Hara, Doctor Meade, Belle Watling and the host of others exactly as every reader has pictured them, living, breathing, real, vital.

From it all, Vivien Leigh emerges as one of the greatest of the great. Her characterization of Scarlett O'Hara is one of the finest portrayals of all time. She IS Scarlett, passionate, reckless, ruthless, selfish, hypocritical, dishonest, but always a thing of flame, beautiful, lovable. The evolution of her character from the carefree days before the war, through the hell of battle-stricken years and the crueller days of reconstruction, America's most tragic era, is an achievement of such compelling artistry that she dominates her every scene, even when she is sharing it with a Clark Gable giving the finest performance of his career as the dashing, unscrupulous, but always fascinating Rhett Butler.

Gable Is Superb

In his portrayal, Gable reaches the heights. With every scene, it becomes more impressively evident that no one else in the playing world today could have matched his interpretation of a role which he fills with such glovelike fitness that it would seem almost to have been created with him in mind.

It is impossible to draw fine distinctions between the efforts of any of those who comprise the lengthy cast. Olivia deHavilland is magnificent as the gentle Melanie. Leslie Howard is superb as Ashley Wilkes. Hattie McDaniel is unforgettable as the faithful, obstreperous Mammy. Ona Munson is swell as Belle Watling, the madame. But so one might speak of everyone in the cast. Not one, but here gives the finest performance he or she ever has offered. Thomas Mitchell is Gerald O'Hara to the life. Cammie King is a wholly captivating Bonnie Blue, Harry Davenport is a perfect Doctor Meade. Laura Hope Crews is a standout as a fluff-headed grande dame.

Fleming Work Perfect

Victor Fleming g s automatically into the ranks of the greatest directors in film annals with his magnificent work on this picture. It is flawless perfection. The late Sidney Howard who, tragically enough, never saw a foot of the film, has left a worthy and memorable monument with his superfine screenplay which so completely grasped the spirit and the atmosphere of the book. Max Steiner, assisted by Lou Forbes, has provided a musical score which is compelling in its melodic beauty and the perfect keying of every scene.

Of the matchless photography, too

"GONE WITH THE WIND"
(Selznick International-MGM)

Producer............David O. Selznick
Director...............Victor Fleming
Screenplay...........Sidney Howard
Based on novel by: Margaret Mitchell.
Photography ....Ernest Haller
Technicolor Associates: Ray Rennahan, Wilfrid M. Cline.
Special Photographic Effects: Jack Cosgrove.
Fire Effects................Leo Zavitz
Musical Score.............Max Steiner
Associate......................Lou Forbes
Production designed by: William Cameron Menzies.
Art Direction...........Lyle Wheeler
Supervising Film Editor: James E. Newcom.

The Players: Vivien Leigh, Clark Gable, Leslie Howard, Olivia deHavilland, Hattie McDaniel, Thomas Mitchell, Barbara O'Neil, George Reeves, Fred Crane, Everett Brown, Zack Williams, Oscar Polk, Victor Jory, Evelyn Keyes, Ann Rutherford, Butterfly McQueen, Howard Hickman, Harry Davenport, Alicia Rhett, Rand Brooks, Carroll Nye, Marcella Martin, Laura Hope Crews, Leona Roberts, Jane Darwell, Albert Morin, Mary Anderson, Terry Shero, Willia McClain, Eddie Anderson, Jackie Moran, Cliff Edwards, Ona Munson, Ed Chandler, George Hackathorne, Roscoe Ates, John Arledge, Eric Linden, Tom Tyler, William Bakewell, Lee Phelps, Paul Hurst, Ernest Whitman, William Sterling, Louis Jean Heydt, Isabel Jewell, Robert Elliott, George Meeker, Wallis Clark, Irving Bacon, Adrian Morris, J. M. Kerrigan, Olin Howland, Yakima Canutt, Blue Washington, Ward Bond, Cammie King, Mickey Kuhn, Lillian Kemble Cooper.

---

much cannot be said. All honor to Ernest Haller, top cameraman, to Ray Rennahan and Wilfrid M. Cline, his Technicolor associates, to Jack Cosgrove for his amazing special photographic effects, to Leo Zavitz for the scenes of the burning of Atlanta which have never been equalled.

All honor, too, to all those others who designed the production, created its stunning sets and provided them with their faithfully correct furnishings and decorations, who provided the costumes or who had anything to do with the making of "Gone With the Wind."

Film Great Event

This picture is an event, the greatest event to date, in motion picture production. One could speak of it endlessly and still not pay it the tribute which is its due. Into it David Selznick has poured the last ounce of matchless production effort. He has given the world a treasure of splendor and living artistry for which it owes him an incalculable debt. It was three and a half years ago that he ventured upon the "Gone With the Wind" path. This triumph has been worth waiting for.

Tales of Hoffman

New York.—Dave Burns, who plays the part of Banjo (Harpo Marx, of course) in "The Man Who Came to Dinner," wrote a letter to Harpo the other day in which he said: "Everywhere I go—the Stork Club, Lindy's, Tavern, El Morocco—every one thinks I'm you. Am sure you wouldn't want me to embarrass you by not tipping and ordering sparingly, send me some money to keep up your front."

●

In a hearty hosannah in praise of "Ninotchka" — which should have been headlined "Broun Discovers Garbo"—Heywood Broun also handed a few reverse English posies to the cinema. "Until the other night," wrote Broun, "I thought the noblest thing the talking pictures had to offer was some shot of a snow-capped peak or a rushing torrent. Now I have seen Greta Garbo, and many of my prejudices and blank spots must go up in smoke. The lady is an artist." Later on in the piece, Heywood heckled: "Always in pictures the spectators get too much of a good thing. I have heard of an institution known as the cutting room, but I wonder if what they slash is one-half as terrible as the stuff they send out."

To quote a playwright with two productions now on Broadway, "This is the most unkindest cut of all!"

●

An associate producer was moaning to a writer about his troubles the other day. He had just received notice that he was to be laid off for a month. The writer listened calmly—but unsympathetically — to the producer's tale of woe. . . . "What are you complaining about?" he finally squelched. "I was out of work for fifteen years—once!"

●

The Institute of Arts and Sciences at Columbia University, which is giving a program of popular lectures at its McMillin Theatre, is including the showing of "The 10 outstanding motion pictures of the double-decade from 1915 to 1935." The selections were made by an informal jury consisting of Dr. Russell Potter, director of Columbia's Division of Motion Picture Study; Wilton A. Barrett, director of the National Board of Motion Picture Review; Iris Barry, curator of the Film Library; Bette Davis; William James Fadiman, story editor for MGM; James Shelley Hamilton, of the National Board of Review; Hal Hode, member of the executive staff of Columbia Pictures; Paul Muni, Frank Nugent, Terry Ramsaye, Gilbert Seldes, Spencer Tracy, King Vidor and Jake Wilk, of Warners. The ten pictures to be shown until the end of February are, in order of preference: "Birth of a Nation," "The Big Parade," "Cabinet of Dr. Caligari," "The Kid," "Nanook of the North," "It Happened One Night," "The Informer," "Potemkin," "Anna Christie" and "Variety."

Hollywood Reporter, *December 13, 1939 (Courtesy of the Academy of Motion Picture Arts and Sciences).*

The Atlanta Premiere of Gone With the Wind (*Photo: Photofest*).

ACKNOWLEDGMENTS

ON THE ROAD TO TARA would not exist without the help and encouragement of L. Jeffrey Selznick and Daniel Mayer Selznick who made available to me all the visual and written materials left by their father, David O. Selznick. That was an open sesame to treasures which rival those collected by the forty thieves, and I am deeply grateful to them.

My thanks also go to Rand Brooks, Fred Crane, Evelyn Keyes, and Ann Rutherford for sharing their memories of acting in *Gone With the Wind* and to Dorothea Holt Redmond for sharing her recollections as a sketch artist on the film.

Since the events that are chronicled in *On the Road to Tara* took place nearly sixty years ago, much of my research for this book was archival. I am extremely indebted to Margaret Howard for allowing me to quote from the letters of her father, Sidney Howard. I also wish to thank David S. Zeidberg of the Department of Special Collections, University Research Library, University of California at Los Angeles, for permission to quote from oral histories housed at the collection, and Anthony S. Bliss, Rare Book Librarian at the Bancroft Library at the University of California, Berkeley, for access to the library's Sidney Howard Collection. I want to express my appreciation to the American Society of Cinematographers for making available audiotapes of their oral histories; and to Alan David Vertrees and Ali Hossein, Editor-in-Chief of The University of Texas Press, for their cooperation.

Much of the research for this book was done in the Selznick Archive at the Harry Ransom Humanities Research Center at the University of Texas at Austin. My splendid tour guide was Dr. Charles Bell, assistant film curator at the Research Center and administrator of the Archive. I could never have found my way through the material without the help of Dr. Bell and of Steve Wilson.

I particularly wish to express my gratitude to David Thomson, author of *Showman: The Life of David O. Selznick* (Alfred A. Knopf, 1992). Mr. Thomson generously shared with me interviews he had done for *Showman* and for the notable 1988 documentary *The Making of a Legend: Gone With the Wind*. Many of the people Mr. Thomson interviewed have died during the intervening decade, and I would not have been able to include their voices in this book without his help. My thanks also go to Jeffrey and Daniel Selznick for providing me with other interviews that were done for *The Making of a Legend*, which they produced.

All material illustrated in this book has been drawn from the Selznick Archive at the Harry Ransom Humanities Research Center at the University of Texas, unless specifically credited to another source in the caption.

I would like to thank William Tomkin, curator of the Fred A. Parrish Collection, for making available candid photographs taken on the set of *Gone With the Wind* by Mr. Parrish, who was the still photographer on the movie.

The members of the Selznick family, in particular, would like to extend their sincere appreciation to Dennis A. Shaw and James Tumblin for graciously allowing portions of their collection to be reproduced in this book, since theirs is considered to be the largest privately owned collection of *Gone With the Wind* costumes, production drawings, and related memorabilia in the United States. Their cooperation has also been greatly appreciated by me and by the publisher, Harry N. Abrams, Incorporated.

My words would have looked very gray on the pages of this book without the exceptional work of Sam Antupit, who designed *On the Road to Tara*. Thank you again, Sam. My thanks also to Beverly Fazio Herter, who edited the text, and to my editor Adele Westbrook, who coordinated all our efforts and made sure that pictures and pages got where they were supposed to go and got there on time. I was also helped in numerous ways by my husband, Richard Harmetz.

Lastly, I would like to thank my son, Anthony Harmetz, who acted as a rigorous and demanding editor on every version of the text from first draft to last.

Notes and Sources

The bulk of the archival material in this book comes from documents in the Selznick Archive at the Harry Ransom Humanities Research Center at the University of Texas in Austin. David Selznick kept almost everything, and the three million pieces of paper in the Archive would fill 2,800 file drawers. Although the documents used have not been individually sourced, they can be found in Boxes 38H, 39H, 177, 180, 181, 185, 191, 193, 305, 411–14, 418, 419, 436–38, 626, 630, 633, 895, 911, 932, 938, 943, 1133, 1139, 1221, 1258, 1260, 1291, 1298, 1592, and 4380. (All illustrations drawn from the Fred A. Parrish Collection are © 1981 by Darlene G. Parrish & William J. Tomkin. All Rights Reserved. Photo Credit: Fred A. Parrish.) (All illustrations from Collection Dennis A. Shaw and James Tumblin are © 1996. All rights reserved.)

Quotations that came from elsewhere are sourced below. In these notes, books are cited by the author's name, title, and page only; full publication information can be found in the bibliography. The words identifying a note are taken from the beginning of the section of the text to which they refer.

Three archives are abbreviated as follows:
DSC/URL/UCLA   Department of Special Collections/University Research Library/
     University of California at Los Angeles
SH/BL/UCB   Sidney Howard papers/Bancroft Library/University of California at Berkeley
MHL/AMPAS   Margaret Herrick Library, Academy of Motion Picture Arts and Sciences

PROLOGUE

16   "David would have told. . . . " Hal Kern, interviewed by Ronald Haver.
16   "For us, the preview. . . . " Irene Mayer Selznick, *A Private View*, p. 218.
16   "extruding energy. . . . " Richard Harwell, ed. "Technical Advisor: The Hollywood Journals of Wilbur G. Kurtz", p. 38.
17   "was thunderous. . . . " Hal Kern, interviewed by Ronald Haver.
21   "We'd have been on it. . . . " Hal Kern, interviewed by BBC.
21   Theatrical earnings of *GWTW* translated into 1995 dollars by Art Murphy, *Variety* financial analyst, interviewed by author.

SCRIPTS

31   "He was a born. . . . " John F. Wharton, *Life Among the Playwrights*, p. 5.
31   "Sidney Howard immediately. . . . " A. Scott Berg, interviewed by author.
32   "The tough part. . . . " Undated letter to David Selznick from Sidney Howard, SH/BL/UCB.
32   "I don't know. . . . " Letter from Sidney Howard to Polly Howard, April 14, 1937, SH/BL/UCB.
32   "It is obvious. . . . " Sidney Howard to David Selznick, February 12, 1937, SH/BL/UCB.
33   "I don't believe. . . . " Irene Mayer Selznick, *A Private View*, p. 158.
33   "He carried no keys. . . . " Ibid., p. 157.
33   "I am only. . . . " Sidney Howard to Sam Marx, June 17, 1937, SH/BL/UCB.
34   "parked in the. . . . " Richard Harwell, ed. "Technical Advisor: The Hollywood Journals of Wilbur G. Kurtz," p. 20.
34   "The quickest way. . . . " Ibid., p. 43.
34   "Yes, I'm through. . . . " Ibid, p. 42.
35   "a brilliant plotter. . . . " Ben Hecht, *A Child of the Century*, p. 482.
39   "It had taken me. . . . " Richard Harwell, Ed., *Margaret Mitchell's Gone With the Wind Letters: 1936–1949*, p. 73.
48   "absolutely forbidden. . . . " A. Scott Berg, *Max Perkins*, p. 369.
48   "And George has continuously. . . . " Susan Myrick, *White Columns in Hollywood*, p. 127.
49   "David wanted me to read. . . . " King Vidor, interviewed by author for *The Making of the Wizard of Oz*.

52   "David, he said. . . . " Marcella Rabwin, interviewed by David Thomson, November 12, 1987.

52   "Selznick and Vic Fleming. . . . " Ben Hecht, *A Child of the Century*, pp. 488–89.

52   "They have done nothing. . . . " Letter from Sidney Howard to Polly Howard, April 5, 1939, SH/BL/UCB.

53   "Less than ever. . . . " Letter from Sidney Howard to Polly Howard, April 12, 1939, SH/BL/UCB.

53   "will put still another. . . . " Letter from Sidney Howard to Polly Howard, April 8, 1939, SH/BL/UCB.

TARA

55   "I insisted I was right. . . . " Richard Harwell, ed., "Technical Advisor: The Hollywood Journals of
        Wilbur G. Kurtz", p. 76.

61   "nothing gorgeous. . . . " Ibid., p. 62.

61   "Maybe a true representation. . . . " Ibid.

61   "I swear these fools. . . . " Susan Myrick, *White Columns in Hollywood*, p. 166.

62   "I believe. . . . " Richard Harwell, ed., *Margaret Mitchell's Gone With the Wind Letters: 1936–1949*,
        pp. 358–9.

62   "If I'm gonna. . . . " Wilbur Kurtz, speech to the Civil War Roundtable in Atlanta, February 20, 1962.

62   "The book is law. . . . " Walter Plunkett's slide lecture, 1981.

68   "They brought a bootmaker. . . . " Ann Rutherford, interviewed by author.

69   "David just wanted. . . . " David Thomson, *Showman*, p. 262.

BURNING

97   "exceedingly beautiful. . . . " Clarence W. D. Slifer, "Creating Visual Effects for G.W.T.W.,"
        American Cinematographer, August 1982.

97   "I stripped them. . . . " William Cameron Menzies speech at the University of Southern California,
        April 10, 1929, printed as "Pictorial Beauty in the Photoplay," *Cinematographic Annual*,
        ed. Hal Hall, 1930.

99   "great ingenuity. . . . " Ibid.

100 "In a Ph.D. thesis. . . . " Alan David Vertrees, "A Single Vision: David O. Selznick and the Film Production
        of *Gone With the Wind*." A book based on material in the thesis will be published by the University
        of Texas Press.

100 "an intermediate process. . . . " Ezra Goodman, "Production Designing," *American Cinematographer*,
        March 1945.

100 "a very analytical. . . . " W. Howe Cameron Menzies, "Cinema Design," *Theatre Arts Monthly*,
        September 1929, pp. 676–83.

101 "Before GWTW started. . . . " Slifer, "Creating Visual Effects for GWTW."

102 "Between the two. . . . " Ridgeway Callow, Oral History, MHL/AMPAS.

102 "He was one of. . . . " Hal Kern, interviewed by Ronald Haver.

103 "it's the first. . . . " Letter from Sidney Howard to Polly Howard, April 21, 1937, SH/BL/UCB.

103 "Sam Goldwyn. . . . " Sidney Howard to Polly Howard, April 25, 1937, SH/BL/UCB.

103 "Slowly we were. . . . " Slifer, "Creating Visual Effects for GWTW."

105 "which meant that every. . . . " Mary Corliss and Carlos Clarens, "Designed for Film: The Hollywood Art
        Director," *Film Comment*, May/June 1978, p. 56.

105 "The matte line. . . . " Slifer, "Creating Visual Effects for GWTW."

105 "As each group. . . . " Slifer, original manuscript for "Creating Visual Effects for GWTW," American
        Society of Cinematographers files.

106 "He was really. . . . " Marcella Rabwin, interviewed by George Wead, April 3, 1987.

106 "David Selznick was a man. . . . " Raymond Klune, Oral History, DSC/URL/UCLA.

106 "That was worked out. . . . " Ibid.

106 "The impressive fact. . . . " Richard Harwell, ed., "Technical Advisor: The Hollywood Journals of
        Wilbur G. Kurtz," p. 90.

107 "The various steel cables. . . . " Ibid., p. 92.

107 "If Eliza crossing. . . . " Ibid., p. 94.

108 "They tested her. . . . " Marcella Rabwin, interviewed by David Thomson, November, 13, 1987.

109 "absolutely modern. . . . " Hal Kern, interviewed by Ronald Haver.

CENSORSHIP

138 "and they thought. . . . " Jack Vizzard, *See No Evil*, p. 64.

144 "Hitler and his. . . . " Karl Lishka, Production Code Administration files, MHL/AMPAS.

144 "In a memorandum. . . . " Joseph Breen, Ibid.

144 "My dear, they want. . . . " Margaret Mitchell, *Gone With the Wind*.

PRODUCTION

149 "But I doubt if Selznick. . . . " Letter from Sidney Howard to Polly Howard, July 15, 1937, SH/BL/UCB.

150 "I'm not keen. . . . " Leslie Ruth Howard, *A Quite Remarkable Father*, p. 254.

150 "the abominable Ashley. . . . " Ronald Howard, *In Search of My Father*, p. 19.

153 "You cannot go. . . . " Marcella Rabwin, interviewed by David Thomson, November 12, 1987.

153 "you really make. . . . " Raymond Klune, Oral History, DSC/URL/UCLA.

153 "Selznick was a nut. . . . " Evelyn Keyes, interviewed by author.

153 "He went by trial. . . . " Ridgeway Callow, Oral History, MHL/AMPAS.

153 "Generally speaking. . . . " Raymond Klune, Oral History, DSC/URL/UCLA.

156 "Now look here. . . . " George Cukor, Oral History, DSC/URL/UCLA.

158 "a blend of. . . . " Victoria Fleming, interviewed by author, 1975.

158 "were a natural. . . . " Budd Schulberg, *Moving Pictures*, p. 396.

160 "He went all back. . . . " Raymond Klune, Oral History, DSC/URL/UCLA.

161 "but Zanuck. . . . " Mary Corliss and Carlos Clarens, "Designed for Film:
    The Hollywood Art Director," p. 57

161 "Selznick was a very hard. . . . " Hal Kern, interviewed by BBC.

166 "Just one climax. . . . " Ronald Howard, *In Search of My Father*.

166 "They were handing her. . . . " Evelyn Keyes, interviewed by author.

166 "Pieces came down. . . . " Rand Brooks, interviewed by author.

167 "He was very aloof. . . . " Ridgeway Callow, Oral History, MHL/AMPAS.

168 "How really astonishing. . . . " Ibid., April 8, 1939.

168 "I thought the stuff. . . . " Sidney Howard to Polly Howard, April 5, 1939, SH/BL/UCB.

168 "I have never. . . . " Ibid., April 18, 1939.

168 "At the end. . . . " Raymond Klune, Oral History, DSC/URL/UCLA.

168 "It happened fourteen. . . . " Ridgeway Callow, Oral History, MHL/AMPAS.

169 "David wanted his Scarlett. . . . " Sunny Lash, interviewed for *The Making of a Legend*.

169 "When I leave school. . . . " Alexander Walker, *Vivien: The Life of Vivien Leigh*, p.32.

169 "I think he looks. . . . " Alexander Walker, *Vivien: The Life of Vivien Leigh*, p. 39.

169 "was the bitch. . . . " Hal Kern, interviewed by BBC.

169 "she was a real pro. . . . " Ridgeway Callow, Oral History, MHL/AMPAS.

169 "She never stopped. . . . " Evelyn Keyes, interviewed by author.

169 "She hurled herself. . . . " Ann Rutherford, interviewed by author.

170 "She was a sweetheart. . . . " Hal Kern, interviewed by BBC.

194 "walked right off. . . . " Ridgeway Callow, Oral History, MHL/AMPAS.

205 "Sam leaned on him. . . . " Ray Rennahan, Oral History of *Duel in the Sun*, DSC/URL/UCLA.

208 "The jig's up. . . . " Irene Mayer Selznick, *A Private View*, p. 265.

208 "I didn't want more. . . . " Ibid., p. 268.

BIBLIOGRAPHY

Behlmer, Rudy, ed. *Memo From David O. Selznick*. New York: Viking, 1972.

———. *Inside Warner Bros. (1935–1951)*. New York: Viking, 1985.

Berg, A. Scott. *Goldwyn*. New York: Alfred A. Knopf, 1989.

———. *Max Perkins*. New York: E.P. Dutton, 1978.

Fitzgerald, F. Scott. *The Last Tycoon*. New York: Charles Scribner's Sons, 1941.

Flamini, Roland. *Scarlett, Rhett, and a Cast of Thousands*. New York: Macmillan, 1975.

Gabler, Neal. *An Empire of Their Own*. New York: Crown, 1988.

Gussow, Mel. *Don't Say Yes Until I Finish Talking*. New York: Doubleday, 1971.

Harmetz, Aljean. *The Making of the Wizard of Oz*. New York: Alfred A. Knopf, 1977.

Harwell, Richard, ed. "Technical Advisor: The Hollywood Journals of Wilbur G. Kurtz,"
   Atlanta Historical Journal, Summer 1978.

———. *Margaret Mitchell's Gone With the Wind Letters: 1936–1949*. New York: Macmillan, 1976.

———. *Gone With the Wind as Book and Film*. Columbia, S.C.: University of South Carolina Press, 1983.

Haver, Ronald. *David O. Selznick's Hollywood*. New York: Alfred A. Knopf, 1980.

Hecht, Ben. *A Child of the Century*. New York: Simon & Schuster, 1954.

Higham, Charles. *Sisters*. New York: Coward-McCann, 1984.

Howard, Leslie Ruth. *A Quite Remarkable Father*. New York: Harcourt, Brace, 1959.

Howard, Ronald. *In Search of My Father*. New York: St. Martin's Press, 1981.

Kahn, E. J., Jr. *Jock: The Life and Times of John Hay Whitney*. Garden City, N.Y.: Doubleday, 1981.

Keyes, Evelyn. *Scarlett O'Hara's Younger Sister*. Secaucus, N.J.: Lyle Stuart, 1977.

Korda, Michael. *Charmed Lives*. New York: Random House, 1979.

Kozarski, Richard. *Hollywood Directors 1914–1940*. New York: Oxford University Press, 1976.

Lambert, Gavin. *On Cukor*. New York: Putnam, 1972.

———. *GWTW: The Making of Gone With the Wind*. Boston: Atlantic-Little, Brown, 1973.

LoBrutto, Vincent. *By Design*. Westport, Ct.: Praeger, 1992.

Marx, Samuel. *Mayer and Thalberg*. New York: Random House, 1975.

Mitchell, Margaret. *Gone With the Wind*. New York: Macmillan, 1936.

Mordden, Ethan. *The Hollywood Studios*. New York: Alfred A. Knopf, 1988.

Myrick, Susan. *White Columns in Hollywood*. Edited by Richard Harwell. Macon, Ga.:
   Mercer University Press, 1982.

Niven, David. *Bring On the Empty Horses*. New York: Putnam, 1975.

Schatz, Thomas. *The Genius of the System*. New York: Pantheon, 1988.

Schulberg, Budd. *Moving Pictures*. New York: Stein & Day, 1981.

Schumach, Murray. *The Face on the Cutting Room Floor*. New York: William Morrow, 1964.

Selznick, Irene Mayer. *A Private View*. New York: Alfred A. Knopf, 1981.

Selznick, L. Jeffrey and Daniel Mayer, Executive Producers; Selznick, L. Jeffrey, Producer; Hinton, David,
   Director; Thomson, David, Writer; *The Making of a Legend: Gone With the Wind, 1988*.

Sennett, Robert S. *Setting the Scene: The Great Hollywood Art Directors*. New York: Harry N. Abrams, 1994.

Sklar, Robert. *Movie-Made America*. New York: Random House, 1975.

Thomas, Bob. *Selznick*. New York: Doubleday, 1970,

Thomson, David. *A Biographical Dictionary of Film*. New York: William Morrow, 1976.

———. *Showman*. New York: Alfred A. Knopf, 1992.

Vertrees, Alan David. "A Single Vision: David O. Selznick and the Film Production of *Gone With the Wind*."
   Ph.D. thesis, Columbia University, 1992.

Vizzard, Jack. *See No Evil*. New York: Simon & Schuster, 1970.

Walker, Alexander. *Vivien: The Life of Vivien Leigh*. New York: Macmillan, 1980.

Wharton, John F. *Life Among the Playwrights*. New York: Quadrangle/The New York Times Book Co., 1974.

INDEX